Linux Thin Client Networks Design and Deployment

A quick guide for System Administrators

David Richards

PUBLISHING

BIRMINGHAM - MUMBAI

Linux Thin Client Networks Design and Deployment

A quick guide for System Administrators

First published: August 2007

Production Reference: 1030807

Published by Packt Publishing Ltd.
32 Lincoln Road
Olton
Birmingham, B27 6PA, UK.

ISBN 978-1-847192-04-2

www.packtpub.com

Cover Image by Andrew Jalali (www.acjalali.com)

Credits

Author

David Richards

Reviewers

Diego Torres Milano

Blaine Hilton

Senior Acquisition Editor

David Barnes

Development Editor

Nikhil Bangera

Technical Editor

Rajlaxmi Nanda

Editorial Manager

Dipali Chittar

Project Manager

Patricia Weir

Project Coordinator

Sagara Naik

Indexer

Bhushan Pangaonkar

Proofreader

Chris Smith

Production Coordinator

Shantanu Zagade

Cover Designer

Shantanu Zagade

About the Author

David Richards is a System Administrator for the City of Largo, Florida. He has been exposed to computer technologies since the day he got his first home computer in the early 1980s. After graduating from college in 1986, he was employed in the manufacturing, distributing, and printing industries. 1992 was the first year that he entered the City's employment, working with UNIX, Linux, and thin clients. He promotes thin clients and open source technology, and enjoys the challenges in their deployment. He is often found in the GNOME IRC channels debugging software and interacting with the developers.

About the Reviewers

Diego Torres Milano is the founder and CTO of COD Technologies Ltd., a company specializing in Information and Communications Technologies (ICT) consultancy services, software development, and Commercial Open Source, mainly in the areas of Server-Based Computing and thin clients. Previously, he has founded and developed the successful PXES Universal Linux Thin Client project, which was then acquired and transferred to another company and was also the base for other thin client projects as well.He has also helped many important global organizations to find the most suitable Free/Libre Open Source Software alternatives, and has dedicated the last 15 years to Unix and Linux consulting, and software development.

For more information about COD Technologies Ltd. and its projects, you can visit `http://codtech.com`.

Blaine Hilton has always been a technology enthusiast from an early age. Blaine owns a business that he started right out of high school, which offers computer and network consulting, web site design/development and web application development. His current interests include expanding the capability of web-based applications and finding applications to use web apps in the real world. Blaine, through his company Blaine's Business Services, Inc. works to combine technology and business skills to provide clients with direct bottom line results.

Blaine has won Young Entrepreneur of the Year for the Northwest Indiana region.

Table of Contents

Preface

It is with interest that the author has an eye on technology when visiting other organizations and also as part of normal daily life. A visit to the local home-improvement or video store will show how expensive client/ server technology has been deployed, where thin clients would easily meet their needs. It's also interesting to the author that a visit to a major computer store chain demonstrates that solid-state computing is known for its stability and reliability. This entire store is devoted to personal computers and networking, and all of their point of sales and inventory systems are on dumb terminals!

Thought has been given to this book in terms of creating something that is well rounded, and meets the needs of small and large organizations. Computer technology is changing all the time, and attempts were made to keep the contents of this book relevant for as long as possible. Items of security are best suited for the System Administrator or integrator of a solution, and will not be discussed much in the chapters. The information covered will give you enough knowledge to understand how the technology works, make decisions about deployment, and then implement a stable work environment.

What This Book Covers

Chapter 1: *Overview of Thin Clients* will give you an overview of what exactly is a thin client, and the different types of models that are available.

Chapter 2: *The Types of Thin Clients* will give you a sample of multiple types of thin clients. Once you have configured your server, you will have to make decisions about which types of hardware to deploy.

Chapter 3: *An Analysis of Costs* will identify key areas to review when considering the financial impact of your thin client plan. This includes hardware acquisition and also staffing costs.

Chapter 4: *The People Issues* will address what might be the hardest part of your deployment: People. Some people are passionate about their software and others are challenged with any workflow changes. It's important to address them as much as possible before, during and after deployment.

Chapter 5: *Considering the Network* will review the network required to run thin clients. Because of the simplicity of the computing deployment, your network too is simplified.

Chapter 6: *Implementing the Server* will cover the steps necessary to design a server for the number of users in your deployment. Also covered will be steps to allow thin clients to log into and run a desktop environment.

Chapter 7: *Implementing the User Software* will provide ideas for software packages that run on Linux, along with their suitability to run over the network to thin clients.

Chapter 8: *Implementing the Thin Clients* reviews the process of considering the operating system to deploy on the devices. Also covered is the interaction with USB devices and speakers.

Chapter 9: *Support* covers three aspects of support. The first is supporting your users, the second is support within your IT staff, and the third is support from software vendors.

Appendix A: This lists out the URLs of the various projects and hardware mentioned in this book.

Appendix B: This takes you through the installation of OpenSUSE.

Conventions

In this book, you will find a number of styles of text that distinguish between different kinds of information. Here are some examples of these styles, and an explanation of their meaning.

Code words in text are shown as follows: "In your custom directory the file `GdmGreeterTheme.desktop` contains the information relevant to the design of the theme."

Any command-line input and output is written as follows:

```
rsh <second_computer> date
```

New terms and **important words** are introduced in a bold-type font. Words that you see on the screen, in menus or dialog boxes for example, appear in our text like this: "Select **Same as Local** to display the graphical login".

 Important notes appear in a box like this.

Reader Feedback

Feedback from our readers is always welcome. Let us know what you think about this book, what you liked or may have disliked. Reader feedback is important for us to develop titles that you really get the most out of.

To send us general feedback, simply drop an email to feedback@packtpub.com, making sure to mention the book title in the subject of your message.

If there is a book that you need and would like to see us publish, please send us a note in the **SUGGEST A TITLE** form on www.packtpub.com or email suggest@packtpub.com.

If there is a topic that you have expertise in and you are interested in either writing or contributing to a book, see our author guide on www.packtpub.com/authors.

Customer Support

Now that you are the proud owner of a Packt book, we have a number of things to help you to get the most from your purchase.

Errata

Although we have taken every care to ensure the accuracy of our contents, mistakes do happen. If you find a mistake in one of our books—maybe a mistake in text or code—we would be grateful if you would report this to us. By doing this you can save other readers from frustration, and help to improve subsequent versions of this book. If you find any errata, report them by visiting `http://www.packtpub.com/support`, selecting your book, clicking on the **Submit Errata** link, and entering the details of your errata. Once your errata are verified, your submission will be accepted and the errata added to the list of existing errata. The existing errata can be viewed by selecting your title from `http://www.packtpub.com/support`.

Questions

You can contact us at `questions@packtpub.com` if you are having a problem with some aspect of the book, and we will do our best to address it.

1
Overview of Thin Clients

In the early 1990s, I had the opportunity to work for a printing company in the Midwest of the United States that needed to stay aggressive in the use of technology to retain its competitive edge. I was there for the shift from dumb terminals to personal computers and client/server technology. In looking back it's interesting to note that this caused a massive change in IT staff workloads. Where previously IT staff were developing software and moving technology ahead, they shifted more and more into a hardware support role and just barely maintaining the infrastructure. Dumb terminals would sit for years and years with no maintenance, and personal computers at desktops needed a lot of attention and care. It's possible to merge the best of both worlds with modern thin clients. One gets the stability of dumb terminals, with the rich graphical interface of personal computers. When computing technology is simplified in this same manner, IT staff can focus once again on development and software support and provide more valuable assistance to the user community.

Theory of Design

The best analogy to thin client technology is to compare it to your telephone and the telephone network. The bulk of what is necessary to make a phone call is provided to you on the network and the telephone in your house is the most basic of devices. A 5, 10, or 20 year old phone will still plug into the wall and continue to work

as it did when it was new. Telephone features that are added are almost always added on the network itself and everyone instantly gains access to them. This is the same manner in which thin clients are deployed. In the case of telephones, features that were once found only on high-end phones are now common place in very inexpensive ones. The same thing is happening with thin clients and more expensive personal computer hardware.

The line is blurring between the hardware of a thin client and a typical personal computer. At the time of this writing, the author is testing a new thin client that runs at 1 GHz, with a 2GB flash drive, and 1GB of RAM. Thin clients aren't as much about the hardware or software as they are about the design. When using a thin client, most of the software processes are run from a centralized computer system. The end user gets the bare minimum of hardware required to display and interact with that software. Only a keyboard, mouse, monitor, and light operating system are placed at the user desktop.

Where It Runs

On a personal computer network, even if the applications are stored on a server, all of the software runs on the hardware at the desktop. This design creates a lot of variables in the run-time environment of your user community. Different patches, hardware levels, and operating systems will cause applications to perform differently.

When thin clients are used, all software processes run from the servers. For the most part what this means is that once you get something stable and working, it's stable and working for all of your users immediately. Patches and upgrades that are applied to the servers are instantly rolled out to all users. Even if the thin clients are of different age and hardware, they are much less prone to peculiarities and differences. In a network with mixed thin clients, a System Administrator can keep one from each of the models, and test them before deployment. Very few issues arise from different types of thin clients, though it's best to keep unique models to a minimum.

Don't Lose Your Memory

Memory management is handled in a completely different manner on thin clients. Significantly less resources can be used when applications are centralized, especially when they are run on Unix/Linux servers. Let's suppose that you desire to deploy an application called 'OpenFoo', which can be run on either Microsoft Windows or Linux. Let's also assume that you have 10 users on your network. For the sake of simplicity, let's calculate the usage, based on the application itself taking 256MB of memory, the user work space taking 10MB of memory, and a small amount (1MB as an example) of thin-client memory to handle remote display over the network.

In a traditional personal computer deployment, 2.66GB of memory is used to deploy this application. The 1MB of remote display memory is not a factor because the application runs locally ((256MB + 10MB) x 10).

The memory usage of the OpenFoo application on personal computer is shown in the following figure.

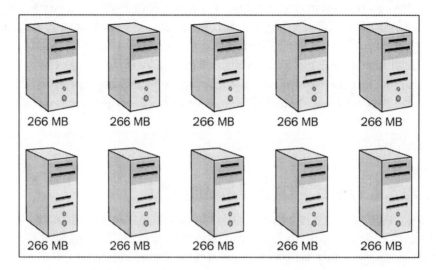

If this scenario is deployed on centralized Microsoft Windows using thin clients, then 2.76GB is required. This slight increase is because of the small amount of memory required on the thin client to handle the video portion of the remote application ((256MB + 10MB + 1MB) x 10).

The memory usage for OpenFoo on centralized Windows is shown in the next figure:

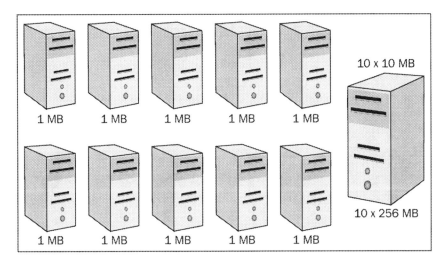

However, when a centralized UNIX/Linux solution is used, only 376MB of memory is required. This is because of the shared memory. When the server detects that a program is already running, it doesn't start another instance of it in memory, and instead simply adds a user space that stores the data specific to the user (10MB + 1MB) x 10) + 256MB). You can see the memory usage for OpenFoo on centralized Linux in the next figure.

This type of memory management allows hundreds of users to run on a single computer system easily, and scales extremely well.

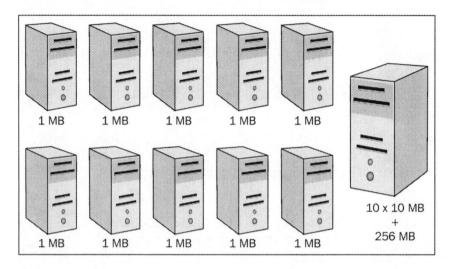

Better Multi-Tasking than a Personal Computer

Another powerful feature achieved with thin clients is how well the system multi-tasks, and how many concurrent applications can be run without degradation. The explanation is very simple: because shared server memory is used and very little thin client memory is used, a great number of applications can be activated at one time.

The next figure represents the OpenFoo application running on a personal computer. In this case, the computer has 512MB of total memory. 256MB of it is consumed by the operating system, and another 256MB is consumed by the OpenFoo itself.

At this point, with one application running it's already out of physical memory and additional applications will be swapped to the hard drive.

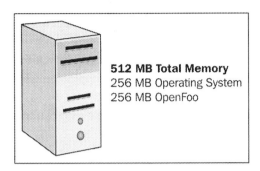

However, the following figure shows memory consumption on a thin client. Assuming once again that the device has 512MB of total memory, and booting the operating system requires 256MB this leaves 256MB for applications. Because each application is only using a small amount of memory to attach to the thin client, a virtually endless number of remote applications can be started. The author has started 30 software packages on a Linux-based thin client with very little noticeable performance penalty.

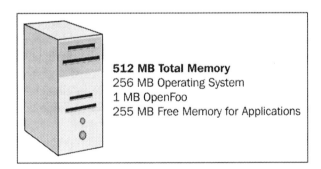

Common Misconceptions

There are a few misconceptions regarding the usage of thin clients. In most cases they seem to permeate from a fear of the unknown, and lack of understanding of the working and deployment of the software. Because you will probably hear of the same issues during your deployment, it's best to be prepared for them and be able to respond accurately.

- **When the server goes down, I won't be able to work.**

  This one is a hold-over from the days of very expensive mainframes and mini-computers. Often, organizations could barely afford to have *one* computer. It was out of the question in years past to have a second one, or any kind of clustering or failover. Especially with centralized Linux servers, it's very easy to add enough servers to cover the event of failure, and split the software workload into small enough pieces that only one software package might be down for a few minutes during a reboot.

- **I won't be able to run application X, Y, or Z.**

  Often, the issue of hardware versus software confuses the user community. They perceive that because Microsoft Windows might be removed from their desktop that now they won't be able to run a certain application that they require. You need to assure people that thin clients actually make it easier to deploy from *any* operating system. You will be able to provide a much greater selection of software. Linux applications will work, mainframe applications will work and yes, their Microsoft applications will work too. Thin clients allow you also to run applications designed for multiple versions of Microsoft Windows concurrently, which is something that cannot be accomplished from a personal computer.

- **Centralized applications must run slower than on a personal computer.**

  In places where one might consider using thin clients, this simply is not true. All basic legacy, specialized, and office software runs perfectly over a network. In fact in the network that I deployed, people have noted that the software seems to run faster via this method than it does on their stand-alone computers. This is because the servers that are built are much faster than a personal computer, have better disk drives, and can be designed to not run out of physical memory, which requires swapping to a hard drive. Because the speed comes from the server and because of reduced costs, focus can be given to upgrades of servers as needed. Normally in larger organizations personal computers are trickled down as new ones arrive. With thin clients, all users have the same speed and experience.

- **I'll lose the ability to gain access to USB devices and CDs.**

  Any devices that can connect to a personal computer can in theory be made to work with a thin client. Sometimes though, it's better to review user workflows and see if there are *smarter* ways for them to work. I have found that once a user is used to physical media they sometimes cannot think of other ways to handle data. It's far easier to email files to other people rather than create static media such as CDs or DVDs. If they are required for your organization, one can connect USB memory sticks and CD/DVD drives to thin clients and gain access to them from host-based applications. You should consider issues of security, stability, and support when weighing exactly what to deploy.

Features Gained in the Thin Design

Thin clients can offer excellent solutions for a diverse set of problems that you might be trying to resolve.

If your primary focus is financial, then under most circumstances thin clients will offer savings. Savings occur from a greatly reduced upgrade cycle and lowered initial installation costs. On the server side, the Linux operating system can offer you a license-free
solution for your users. It also provides an ever increasing amount of open-source software such as the OpenOffice productivity suite, the Evolution email package and many more. In the case of my current employer, a solution has been provided to provide a basic set of applications to all of the users. Login authentication, desktop, email, word processing, and Internet access are all provided with a Linux-based open-source methodology. All, without licenses!

If your primary focus is productivity, gains can be achieved using thin clients as well. Anecdotal evidence suggests that a lot of user time is lost due to personal computers on desktops. At first this statement might sound a bit odd, but not when you consider the 'other things' that the user community does with its personal computers. What a thin client deployment does is remove the hardware and operating system elements from a user's normal day-to-day tasks. Instead of having to troubleshoot problems or experiment with settings, they simply are given a stable environment with software that just works.

If your primary interest is staffing, thin clients will provide a change in focus from desktop maintenance to end-user software support and to future technology research and development. A visitor to a thin client solution will be amazed at the lack of support calls. This is because a lot of resources are used to simply maintain personal computer desktops and associated complexities. Often, problems cannot be handled over the phone and have to be handled by visiting the problematic hardware. In organizations with many buildings, it's easy to see how avoiding this type of maintenance will save a lot of staff time.

Summary

It's difficult to precisely describe how thin clients will fit into your organization because of the many unique needs of each industry, business, or government. My current employer has been using this design for nearly 15 years, and has proven that these design goals can not only be met but also a working solution can be provided. 700 users and 500 workstations can easily be handled with a very small IT staff. The servers are stable, reliable, and fast. A server duty cycle of 3 years and a desktop thin client duty cycle of 10 years have been proven to work well. Open-source software has become robust enough for deployment and stable enough to enjoy weekends off without the ever present sound of a beeper.

2

The Types of
Thin Clients

A surprising diversity of thin clients is available and should be considered. Hardware should be deployed based on user requirements, staff skills, and available funding. My viewpoint is that wireless devices should only be deployed in cases where users require absolute mobility. Thin clients that run at 100Mb or 1 GB and are plugged into a network jack will always be less support intensive and not require any server-side bandwidth-management software. In the sections that follow, the various types of thin clients are described. A summary of pros and cons is provided, along with a model that fits into the described category.

Proprietary Operating Systems

In years past, this type of thin client was far more common. Manufacturers of thin clients would first develop the hardware and then create their own operating system. These devices download a minimal operating system and configuration files via TFTP and then boot and present a menu of systems that are available for login. The biggest benefit to this type of thin client is the fact that changes are instantly picked up by all devices the next time that they are booted. They are very stable because all components come from one manufacturer. However, because of the nature of the closed operating system and a lack of source code, it's impossible to make custom changes or modify the way they function. Additional drivers cannot be added for new types of keyboards and mice that come on the market. These devices are still available on the used market and can be had for just a few dollars each. In a financial pinch, they still work and can be deployed and provide a basic workstation for users. The market has moved away from these closed systems, however, and nearly all of the manufacturers are shipping devices that run the Linux or Windows operating system.

Pros

- Very stable.
- Operating system is perfectly mated to hardware.
- These operating systems are very light and boot quickly.

Cons

- Once manufacturer stops producing upgrades or goes out of business, no way to modify devices.
- No source code means you aren't able to customize.

One example of this type of thin client is the NCD Explora 450 device. While the hardware specs are very tame by the standards of today, they still can provide a 16-bit color, 1024x768 basic desktop.

This device is pictured in the figure below:

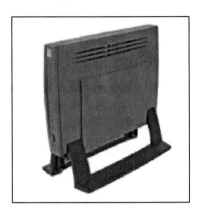

Windows Embedded Devices

Many thin clients running Windows XP embedded have been coming in the market. They are a simple form of regular personal computer, except that they have a small flash drive in place of a regular hard drive. They boot, and then the desktop appears from which connections to Citrix Metaframe or Windows Terminal Services can be formed. Your software applications can be run from centralized computers. Certain license requirements for Microsoft Windows might also be met by running this operating system at the desktop. In my view, this design is very limiting when you wish to deploy software on other operating systems, or more specifically when you want to use X windows as your transport. Windows XP embedded does not natively support connections to Linux servers, and probably would require additional software to be purchased. Some have attempted to install packages on this embedded operating system and have had trouble with libraries being missing. One also has to weigh the very small size of the flash device and loading additional software locally might be beyond the scope of what can be done on a 1 or 2GB flash hard drive. Similar to the proprietary operating systems mentioned in the previous section, you have no source code for these devices. Since you cannot normally make major changes to them, you might have problems in the future getting any upgrades to install if the vendor drops your particular model. Another issue to consider on these devices is viruses and spyware. I have personally seen an XP-based thin client device placed on the Internet, and infected by a virus within 30 minutes. As you deploy your solution, you have to consider ways to keep them from getting infected and the fact is most anti-virus software will not fit on the small flash drives. The flash drives can be write protected, and a reboot in this case will restore it back to the defaults. However, this causes user frustration and unnecessary down time.

Pros

- Potentially some licensing benefits when using Microsoft products where end-user client access license is required.

- Very similar to Windows XP which might aid in organizations with staff already trained.

Cons

- No source code, which makes it more difficult to customize.

- Still prone to viruses and spyware.

- More limited connectivity in mixed operating system environments and when you want to use X windows.

One example of this type of thin client is the Neoware e90. This device supports 32-bit color up to 1600x1200. This device is pictured in the following figure:

Linux Devices

Thin clients are available that run the Linux operating system. Based on its very nature, Linux is easy to customize and many software applications are available for installation on these devices. Since many of those packages are open source, they are license free which can provide significant cost savings. A Linux thin client can be deployed with the following connectivity methods:

- X windows — It's already built into the operating system and provides a transport for X windows applications.

- Telnet — Applications like xterm or gnome-terminal can be used to provide VT100 or ANSI support to legacy Unix/Linux systems and character-based applications.

- 3270 — The excellent open-source application X3270 can be used to provide connectivity to IBM Mainframes.

- Citrix — A native client is available directly from Citrix that runs on Linux.

- RDP — The open-source application Rdesktop can be used to gain access to Microsoft operating systems via RDP.

- Browser — The Firefox browser runs on Linux, and can be used to gain access to web-based applications.

It's clear that many options are available for Linux-based thin clients.

Pros

- Very customizable.
- Very stable.
- License free.
- Many open source applications can be loaded.

Cons

- Possible staff issues related to new operating system if your location is primarily using Microsoft Windows.

- The more a device is customized, the greater level of support of those units must be absorbed.

An example of this thin client is the HP t5725 device. This device ships with a pre-installed version of Linux. It also can be customized greatly and many flavors of Linux can be loaded. An interesting feature on this hardware is the option to add an expansion slot that provides the ability to add generic PCI cards. This allows you to add network or video cards, and provide upgrades for future technology.

The next figure shows this model.

Wireless Devices

Another category of thin clients that might possibly meet your needs is a wireless tablet. These devices are designed to be carried in your hand, and are normally accessed via a stylus pen. While not all of these tablets are Linux-based, they are very simple to configure and can be set up to gain access to Linux or Windows applications on your servers. Some of these devices are designed to run with the Windows CE or Windows Mobile operating system, which provides an instant on design and can be used very quickly. Since no software is loaded locally, they are very easy to configure and use on your network, and are normally write-protected. Any settings or changes made by the user are instantly reset when the unit is powered off and on again. Stylus pens provide mouse support, and often hand writing recognition is included. Because these devices are designed to be wireless they almost always have 802.11 support, and wireless broadband cards can be added if you so desire.

Pros

- Very light operating systems boot quickly.
- Very simple to configure.
- Excellent for use by people while walking or standing, and for those who need to write with a pen.
- Allow roaming desktops and easy-to-gain access to all of your software from anywhere.

Cons

- Not as easy to use when a keyboard is expected or desired.
- Not as easy to customize or make changes, unless they are Linux based.
- In the case of centralized computing, when no wireless connection method is available, cannot get to servers.

One example of this type of thin client is the Airspeak Flair. This device runs the Windows CE. This operating system supports the Citrix client, which can be used to gain access to server-side applications.

The Flair is pictured in the following figure.

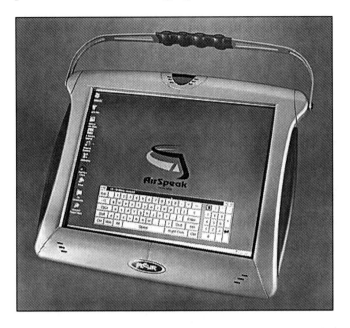

Handheld Devices

One interesting thin client that can be deployed is a handheld device. The screen resolution of these devices has improved and is now able to support running host-based applications. Having run a full GNOME desktop remotely, and tested applications such as the Evolution email client on just such a device, I can say that this solution would not be ideal for a user who uses software for an extended period of time, but is excellent for gaining quick access to your desktop and files. It also can be used in conjunction with client/server applications and your enterprise email packages. Often these devices are already in use in organizations and can easily be absorbed and used as a thin client.

Pros

- Small footprint fits in your pocket.
- Provides complete access to host-based applications.
- Can be used with other client/server applications.

Cons

- Small footprint screen is hard to see.
- Applications are very tiny and widgets are hard to move with stylus.

One example of this type of thin client is the HP hx2700 iPAQ. This device supports 320x240 resolutions and a Citrix client can be deployed. The hx2700 is pictured in the next figure.

Summary

Many types of thin clients were discussed in this chapter. It is important when making decisions to be aware of and consider all options. In most organizations that deploy thin clients, a desktop and then a remote or wireless model will have to be selected. Thin clients running Linux provide excellent functionality and are the best of the options for customizations. They also should give you the best ability to make changes in the future and change peripherals during the projected duty cycle. These devices are normally shipped with an already-installed version of Linux, which can be used should you decide not to create your own build. The diversity of devices creates many exciting possibilities and guarantees a solution that will fit your needs.

3

An Analysis of Costs

There are many reasons why organizations consider thin clients. One of the biggest for you could very well be cost savings. Numerous studies have come out concerning the use of thin clients and centralized computing. Some studies will present information to lead you to believe that moving away from Microsoft products will save you money. Others will warn you to consider the Total Cost of Ownership (**TCO**) and that there might not be savings. What's interesting is that the later usually seem to be studies funded by Microsoft. However, no studies that I have seen have indicated that thin clients are more expensive than client/server computing. While certainly operating system choices can be debated, the issue of lowered costs based on centralized computing is already settled.

Anticipated Costs

Based on the uniqueness of each organization, it would be impossible to exactly calculate the savings for your deployment in these pages. What can be provided is a set of charts and concepts that can be applied to your design. Without a doubt, a move to thin clients from a personal computer network will save you money. A move to Linux on the servers could also provide you significant savings.

Reuse of Current Personal Computers

In the case of already deployed personal computers, one might be tempted to reuse them as thin clients until the end of their duty cycle. According to my opinion this path should be taken only after careful analysis. Retaining a spinning hard drive and a thick licensed operating system is still very support intensive. It's likely that the desktop support costs will still be higher while running it as a thin client than simply replacing the hardware. But this option is certainly available and should be considered.

Possible Reductions in Server Counts

My current employer has had a number of other organizations come in for a facility tour. Those that were running the client/server environment often make a very interesting observation; centralized computing running Linux *reduced* the number of servers required to run enterprise solutions. One would normally assume the reverse to be true, but interestingly, this comment has been made repeatedly. It's my belief that this is related to the efficiency of the Linux operating system, which provides excellent scaling capabilities. It is also been observed that organizations with Microsoft Windows think in terms of **servers** for functions instead of **processes**. Server creep seems to be more prevalent running on Windows, which is interesting because all computer power has in theory been pushed to the desktop.

The following scenario is provided to demonstrate a possible deployment to 600 desktops using the Linux operating system on servers. In this case, it's projected that 400 concurrent users will be logged in at any time, 300 of them using email, 200 using word processing and 100 of them using a web browser. Following is an example of the server costs.

Server Legend

A realistic deployment for the requirements specified in the previous paragraph would be 6 total servers. This would be adequate to run the 400 concurrent users. The projected duty cycle of the servers is 4 years. If the Linux operating system and open-source software are used, nearly all of your cost is hardware. There are no user licenses to buy for the operating system and applications. Hardware maintenance contracts are not included and would be present in either case.

One possible server breakdown would be:

- 2 desktop servers for authentication and to provide icons and menus. 2 servers are required to provide fail-over. Having 2 servers in a cluster eliminates the 'if the server goes down, everyone is down' argument. 400 concurrent users are split evenly between the servers.

- 1 email server to run 300 concurrent users.

- 1 word processing server to run 200 concurrent users.

- 1 web surfing server to run 100 concurrent users.

- 1 generic 'back-end' server to run databases, and process email messages and provide a post office.

- Server cost is estimated at 30,000 dollars, which is the current price for a high-end quad processor rack-mounted server at the time of this writing.

Year	Server Costs
1	180,000.00
2	.00
3	.00
4	.00
5	180,000.00
6	.00
7	.00
8	.00
9	180,000.00
10	.00
Total	**540,000.00**

Thin Client versus Client/Server Anticipated Costs

One of the most difficult concepts to convey to those that are looking for cost savings is the issue of buying a thin client versus a personal computer. It's a common perception that a personal computer 'does more' because it's able to run software locally. Running applications at the desktop, however, causes performance to be dictated not by the speed of the servers but by the local CPU. Because of this issue, upgrades are perpetual and constant. When discussing these costs, it's helpful to build a chart showing a long term cost strategy. It's also very helpful to go to your local library and get a 3-year and then 6-year old copy of your favorite PC magazine so that you can clarify exactly how quickly hardware becomes obsolete.

The following tables show one possible scenario, which describes cost of a thin-client deployment versus that of personal computers. It's common for the duty cycle of a personal computer to be 3 years, while that of a thin client can be extended to 8 years. This is the chart that will provide comfort for those who perceive that there is only a slight cost difference between thin clients and personal computers. Once a complete review is done, it's easy to see the savings. For the sake of demonstration, we will assume the cost of each thin client to be 500 dollars, and the cost of each personal computer to be 800 dollars. The organization in the example requires 600 devices. Computer monitors are not included in the chart because they are required in either deployment.

Thin Client Legend	Personal Computer Legend
600 devices, purchased in the first year at 500 dollars each. No additional upgrades are required during the 10 year duty cycle. 1000 dollars a year is added in years 2-10 to replace approximately 50 mouse and keyboard failures at 20 dollars.	With the assumption that personal computers are already deployed, roughly 1/3 will be replaced each year to provide a 3 year duty cycle. 200 devices per year are replaced at 800 dollars each. Mouse and keyboard failures are not calculated because they are replaced every 3 years.

Year	Thin Client Costs	Personal Computer Costs
1	300,000.00	160,000,00
2	1,000.00	160,000.00
3	1,000.00	160,000.00
4	1,000.00	160,000.00
5	1,000.00	160,000.00
6	1,000.00	160,000.00
7	1,000.00	160,000.00
8	1,000.00	160,000.00
9	1,000.00	160,000.00
10	1,000.00	160,000.00
Total	309,000.00	1,600,000.00

Project Staffing Size and Changes

A change in an organization to thin client computing might possibly alter the dynamics of computer staff and hence should be considered. In a personal computer deployment, the staff is often 'middle heavy', which means that the bulk of the staff is often working on the computers at desktops. This type of maintenance is time consuming and tedious but is so common now that it's difficult to imagine a different deployment dynamic. When working with thin clients, that middle tier of hardware specialists is removed at the expense of possibly hiring an additional System Administrator. Because the servers are used heavily and by everyone, skills are required to maintain and tune the software packages and operating system.

The best way to determine staffing costs is to review the current makeup of staff, and then make an estimate of how those resources will change. The following charts indicate one possible staff allocation in a personal computer deployment with 600 devices, and then the corresponding people required after a shift to thin clients. Salaries are estimated and should be replaced with your actual numbers. Management and networking staff is not included, as they will be consistent in either scenario. It is common to have 1 Personal Computer

Technician for every 75 computers, and that number is used in the following example.

Job Descriptions — Personal Computer Deployment	Annual Salary
Systems Administrator	60,000.00
Personal Computer Technician (1)	35,000.00
Personal Computer Technician (2)	35,000.00
Personal Computer Technician (3)	35,000.00
Personal Computer Technician (4)	35,000.00
Personal Computer Technician (5)	35,000.00
Personal Computer Technician (6)	35,000.00
Personal Computer Technician (7)	35,000.00
Personal Computer Technician (8)	35,000.00
Help Desk / Software Support (1)	30,000.00
Help Desk / Software Support (2)	30,000.00
Help Desk / Software Support (3)	30,000.00
Help Desk / Software Support (4)	30,000.00
Total	**460,000.00**

With the same number of thin clients, one additional Systems Administrator is added, the eight Personal Computer Technicians are eliminated, and the Help Desk staff is reduced by one. The reason for these changes is because each desktop is identical, so specialized staff is not required to troubleshoot hardware problems. Help Desk staff can simply take a new thin client to the desk when one fails. There is a greatly reduced number of calls to the Help Desk, and the bulk of the calls are related to software issues. The next table shows one possible example of staff to support 600 thin clients.

Job Descriptions — Thin Client Deployment	Annual Salary
Systems Administrator	60,000.00
Systems Administrator	60,000.00
Help Desk / Software Support (1)	30,000.00
Help Desk / Software Support (1)	30,000.00
Help Desk / Software Support (1)	30,000.00
Total	**210,000.00**

Other Cost Savings to Consider

Whenever I have met with people that were considering a change to either Linux or thin clients, it's always been a pleasure to see their eyes light up when they realize the expensive and time-consuming processes that can be simply eliminated with thin clients. The costs so far have been related to the physical hardware and personnel staffing. The uniqueness of each deployment prohibits formulae for this calculation, but the reader should consider these items that will have much lower costs:

- Operating system licenses
- Licensed applications replaced by their open-source equivalent
- Ghosting type software applications used to create systems
- Desktop anti-virus packages
- Vehicular and travel costs of support staff
- Downtime costs
- Network breach costs
- Restoration costs of documents not saved correctly
- Costs of lost documents not backed up correctly by users

Summary

It should be mentioned again that it would be impossible to produce numbers in a book that will match the exact specifications of your computing environment. But the three major sections describing servers, desktop devices, and staffing should be good enough examples that will help you calculate your own savings. I am confident that in nearly all deployments, significant savings can be achieved and a much better level of support provided.

4

The People Issues

With all that you will be considering in your deployment, the most important and difficult will be 'people-related issues'. It is important to not underestimate the impact that people will have on the project. My experience in thin-client deployment over a number of years helps me sort the issues into several categories and address them in a manner that will maintain a level of professionalism while ensuring that the deployment is as successful as possible. You will not be able to please the entire user community, but before you begin you have to be at peace with those right facts and do the best that you can.

Executive and Management Issues

Without the support of Management, you will probably not have a successful deployment. Consider your organizational chart and meet with all those who are in a position to put their blessing on your project. Some basic techniques in approaching them have proven to be effective.

Initial Project Meeting

The most basic issue to consider is if Management really wants a change. Do not pitch technical merits, because generally they will not have any interest. What they will understand is how this change will increase productivity in your organization. Ensure that they understand that there will be some bumps, and that most of problems will be people related. Clarify for them that they will receive complaints from some users, and that is part of the normal process. The technology works and is stable, but any changes made to your computer environment will cause some people grief. Review with them estimated cost savings, and clarify that they are estimates and might change as things progress. But the strength of thin client computing is that you can estimate costs pretty closely because even if your applications need additional horsepower before the retirement date of your server, one piece of hardware is easily swapped and upgraded. In this case you won't have to perform upgrades to individual workstations. Review with them the staffing changes that will happen because of the deployment. Do not oversell the staff changes; some settling of staff will occur after you are finished and fine tuning can be handled at that point. If after this initial meeting they have a positive view, proceed with developing a comprehensive implementation schedule.

Implementation Schedule

The implementation schedule will be similar to the initial plan that you took to Management, except it will contain more detailed information and provide them with a schedule. Make sure that any non-technical ideas submitted by Management are worked into your plan. There is a perception often that computer professionals do not listen to the user community. It's very important that those people that make the decisions feel that their input was heard, and used. The schedule should include a detailed analysis of information dissemination and training schedules. If the primary focus is cost savings, then checkpoints should be made where they will begin to see the money being saved. Normally in year one comes a lot of stabilization of your environment and greatly reduced number of support calls. In year two, you should begin to see cost savings. That is when a thin client environment should require no great expenses as compared to the personal computer environment that you replaced, which would have required a scheduled upgrade of workstations and associated costs of installation. Next up is your deployment.

Deployment

The most important issue to remember during the actual deployment is communication. Ensure that you continue to give them frequent updates. Some Managers want them often, some want them infrequently and some will only want to be alerted to problems. Figure out where your Managers fall in and then provide them the amount of information they require. Give them lists of training classes, and complete information on who did and who did *not* attend. There is a strong connection between training and those users that complain. Your documentation will be your saviour.

Often, Managers do not have a lot of interaction with the computer system that you are being asked to upgrade. But no matter how much they use it, ensure that they are given a thin client immediately and allowed to use the new system for whatever software functions that they require. Solicit their feedback and work very carefully to keep them happy. If they can use it and see that it works, the complaints of users will be greatly silenced.

User Community Issues

With Management on board with the project, the user community issues will be significantly easier. The three components of a thin client deployment are technical, administrative, and user experience. Most users do not care about the technical nor administrative issues and therein is the core problem. Many users have memorized their software and workflow instead of learning how pieces work, and when individual steps change they will often blame the technology and rarely admit that in fact their own skills could use improvement. There are some solutions that greatly aid in solving these problems.

Initial Feedback

Once Management has approved the project, meet with representatives of the user community and review your plan with them and ask them for feedback and ideas. They know their co-workers, and often know their habits and techniques better than you do. When they realize that the change is coming from the 'top down', they will realize that failure of the user community will reflect poorly on them.

Communication

Faithfully, provide information to the user community. It's sometimes disheartening to review how few people actually read the email messages that you send out. One idea that works well is to record exactly which people read the messages that you sent, and get that information back to Management. Another method to explore is to send messages to key contacts in each of the sections of your organization and have them send out the information on their own. Sometimes, more people will read email when it comes from someone they know, instead of the 'computer people'. These contacts will see first-hand the delivery process of email, and see which of their staff are not reading the messages. Instead of it being your problem, it becomes their problem to resolve.

Desktop Training

If you are moving away from Microsoft Windows and moving to Linux on the desktop, the user community will require training. As computer professionals, basic issues like cascading menus and file managers are very simple. But for those that memorize certain functions, or have created shortcuts this will prove very frustrating. Desktop training should include the following basics:

- Selecting the correct server to pick from a chooser.
- How to log into the system; possibly you might have no passwords on the personal computers that you are replacing, so, this will all be new to them.
- How to customize the desktop, including how to change wallpapers, change fonts, and change themes.
- How to use the file manager and find documents and files.
- How to launch applications.
- How to log off the server.
- How to correctly shut down the thin client.

One concept that works well is to show them features and software that you are deploying that were previously not available on their personal computer. A good example of this might be the Beagle search system, which runs on Linux. During this training you will discover features and items that are being used that possibly are new to you. Make sure that you provide them with solutions that do the same thing on your thin clients when possible.

During the past years I've been giving presentations and thin-client demos in hundreds of companies around the world. And the single thing that captivated most of the audiences during live demos was booting a thin client. What I did was, started a session (using a stateless protocol RDP, ICA, NX) and started to work in an office document. In the middle of the editing, I disconnected the thin client and removed all the connectors (keyboard, mouse, net, etc.), took a brand new thin client from a box, and connected it again. I then booted it and restarted the session. And when the document appeared with the cursor blinking at the same point they were amazed. Sometimes, Windows users are so accustomed to lose their work that this is enough to give them another perspective of thin clients.

Application Training

If you are deploying additional open-source software packages at the same time as the thin clients, make sure that each has its own training class. Quick and simple classes that review too much technology are not effective. Often, your internal computer staff are not the best people to teach the classes. If your budget allows for professional training, it is highly encouraged that you use this. There are instructors who specialize in open-source software such as OpenOffice.org. If you are able, buy commercially available laminated cards that contain tips and shortcuts. It's not always possible to provide training for all employees, but if you can, *offer* everyone training and keep track of who declined.

Desktop Bling

One issue the I have noted is that some of the deepest resentment to losing a personal computer at a desktop is losing the ability to customize it as they wish. This is one of those issues that they will never mention in any meetings. Doing so will make it appear as if they are spending too much time tinkering in the eyes of Management. But face it, they do. I have observed a greater desire to move to new technology when items are installed on the server that allow them to make minor customizations and call the desktop their own. These items include fonts, wallpapers, and themes. Also seasonal applications such as Xsnow installed on the server will go a long way to increasing positive views. As trivial as these seem to you during deployment, they are very important to the user community.

Issue Tracking Software

Once the deployment begins, make sure that you keep track electronically of all of your support calls. Sometimes hallway conversations that you encounter mushroom into serious problems down the road if they are not handled. So many things will be on your mind and you will be very busy, and it's important not to let problems slip through the cracks. Tracking all of these calls will also provide you with a method to review issues months or years after they occur. The user community will often forget the details of calls and if you have recorded the issue and the corresponding solution they will not be able to come back with incorrect information. Issue tracking software also provides an excellent tool to keep track of problem employees, and to do research on which employees should be sent to additional training.

Open Source CDs

Even if you are deploying open-source applications on Linux, most of your user community will probably have Microsoft Windows or Mac OS/X at home. One excellent side feature of open-source software is that it producers are not trying to lock you into a particular type of computer and it is ported to all operating systems. It is suggested that packages such as the Evolution email client, the Firefox browser and the OpenOffice.org productivity suite be downloaded for your users for all platforms and put on CD to take home. Once they begin using these packages at home, they will resist them less at work.

Summary

All of these examples and ideas will allow you to cover the people issues as much as possible. The basics of deployment are to always solicit feedback and offer as much training as possible recording exactly who attended and who did not. You will not be able to make everyone happy, but as long as Management sees that you made every reasonable attempt to accommodate everyone they should be pleased as the project proceeds.

5

Considering the Network

Much information already exists concerning methods for deploying networks and hardware. We shall try to clarify differences between using a network with personal computers and thin clients with the help of anecdotes. Certain designs have also proven to be very stable and provide the best possible solution.

Primary Network

Your first thought might be that your current network will work fine with thin clients and that is entirely possible. But your network might be something that has grown through the years and is not that well designed. Your implementation of thin clients then might be a good time to review the design and make upgrades as needed.

Personal Computers versus Thin Clients

Based on conversations with some hardware vendors, it's clear that most of the testing is done with the expectation that personal computers will be deployed.

The biggest difference is in how the two platforms use the network. When running a personal computer, often software applications are stored on network servers. When you activate an icon, the network pushes the executable down to your PC. Once downloaded into memory, the application runs and then very little interaction takes place until you save a file. Or in other cases, the executables are on the local PC, and network activity is not used until files are saved. If an executable takes a few seconds longer to download, you won't really notice it when using a personal computer. Some networking devices seem better designed for efficiency of download instead of being designed for the smaller and more plentiful packets of network computing. When you activate a software application on a thin client, the presentation of the user interface is pushed to you from the server, and then all keystrokes and mouse activity are transmitted back and forth to the server in real time. The network needs to be very fast, have low latency, and be configured to pass packets immediately to the servers.

Network Design

For implementing your network, the network backbone should be Gigabit if possible. Obviously if your solution is for only a small number of users, this might not be required. Ideally fibre optic lines are then run to each of the wiring closets, and each switch should have it's own line. It is advisable to avoid daisy-chaining the switches together in order to avoid any kind of contention between them. The servers are all plugged into the backbone at Gigabit as well. If a server is required away from a centralized computer room, then it is better to run a separate line instead of plugging it into a switch that will be shared with thin clients. It's important to keep the data paths solidly designed so that all of your real-time interaction will not be delayed.

X windows, RDP, or Citrix are used to display the user presentation. This means that the software is running on the server, but the image of that software is transmitted over the network. It's important that a strong network exists or repaints of windows will be slower and feel sluggish. This issue will cause people problems, with perceptions that a personal computer can run software faster than a network. A correctly designed network will provide excellent response time and the user community should not even see a difference.

Font servers are used to distribute fonts to users. A font server is just a process or application that runs on the server. When a user requests a font, it's sent over the network to the thin client and made available to them immediately. The strength of this design is that all your employees will have the same fonts and while sharing documents, they will render exactly the same way no matter from where you log into the network. Anyone that has shipped documents between personal computers with different fonts, will greatly appreciate this design. When the network is configured correctly, font download and interaction is immediate and undetected by the user community.

NFS mounts are used to connect disk drives between Linux servers. This allows applications to share data between the various servers on your network. Response time needs to be excellent to provide very fast file saves and retrievals, at the same time avoiding applications that lock or timeout while trying to interact with files.

A review of the possible network problems is provided in the following table:

Networking Issue	Symptom(s)
X windows	Slow repaints of user interfaces
RDP	Lockups
Citrix	Disconnections
Font Servers	Slow repaints
	Wrong fonts in applications
Thin Client	Slow keyboard response
	Disconnections
	Slow repaints
NFS Mounts	Lockups
	Slow response in saving files

Remote Sites

It would be wonderful if Gigabit could be run to all of your facilities. But the truth is that often you are not able to deploy that speed, because of cost or physical locations of buildings. Once networking speeds get below 100 Megabit, you will no longer be able to use native X windows and must consider deploying products that compress presentation data. Microsoft RDP will do this, along with Citrix Metaframe, tight-VNC, and NX/Nomachine.

Most of the products the author has tested that compress data seem to become usable around 100K of speed. Dialup connections will work, but repaints will be tedious and not very efficient. A good formula to use is to multiply the number of concurrent users at each remote site by 100 to get a rough estimate of bandwidth required. Using this formula, 3 concurrent users would require roughly 300K of bandwidth. Remember too, that very possibly print jobs will be running on the same circuit, which will consume bandwidth as well. The user community will perceive 'slowness' mostly in the user presentation itself. Print jobs that take a bit longer are not normally noticed. So, one might consider running two circuits to remote sites and splitting the user sessions on one, and the print jobs on the other. That way if massive print jobs are sent, the users won't notice and can continue working. It should be noted as well that some bandwidth management products such as Citrix have designed their software to support printer connectivity that is also compressed.

The most important issue with remote sites is stability and uptime. When you centralize all of your software, it's critical that the network be available or users will not be able to log into the servers and do their job. Many people do not care how it works, just that it's reliable. Consider all of your options such as T1 connections, DSL, and cable modems and then select the solution that seems like the best fit. One effective method is to create a list of all available networking methods, and then create a chart that clearly spells out the features and speed available within each category. As the line becomes cheaper, it normally becomes slower. The decision makers need to understand that at a certain point presentation and software application speed will start to degrade. It is also important to obtain from the vendor exact service levels for each of the connection methods. Commercial and business lines often will guarantee a minimum amount of bandwidth. Regular home-use circuits often are rated for 'burst rates' and run considerably slower than the specified rate.

Some remote users will be using wireless connections. They too will require an application that will perform compression, and should be considered as well. Cellular wireless broadband is providing plenty of bandwidth these days to run with centralized computers.

Thin Client Network Connections

Once you have performed the steps as outlined previously, you will need to finalize your design for the thin clients themselves. If your current deployment is only capable of 10 Megabit, you will definitely want to upgrade the wiring and move to a minimum of 100 Megabit. 100 Megabit provides plenty of bandwidth for very crisp response time from the servers, and mouse and user interface response is excellent. At the time of this writing, running Gigabit to the desktop has not been tested by the author; but if your thin clients support that speed that is an excellent buffer and should provide even greater capabilities. If users are using devices such as laptops, always encourage them to use a wired connection in the office. In the case of X windows, it will avoid having to use a licensed bandwidth compression interface.

At the time of this writing, Gigabit connections to the desktop are becoming more and more commonplace. If part of your deployment is a redesign of the network, run the highest-rated wiring that you are allowed. The author is anticipating that Gigabit thin clients will become available very shortly. More and more software is making use of the 3-dimensional capabilities of thin client video cards, and each step in this direction requires additional bandwidth.

Testing the Network

Anyone that has supported users knows that often they will discover things that the technical staff never anticipated. It's important to turn that into a positive, and isolate as many problems as possible before final deployment. It's effective to place a few thin clients at each of your sites, and on each of the networking technologies that you have selected and perform their regular day-to-day duties. Some types of connections such as X windows sessions are not stateless, and will drop if the network under-performs. If you are considering a new vendor for networking hardware, they should allow you to install demo devices and test them on your infrastructure. Be mindful that sales people sometimes over sell their products or don't understand exactly your design goals, so a real-world test with their hardware before major purchases is always a good idea.

Summary

In this chapter we see that though the complexity of networking cannot be stated strongly enough, it is important to design a rock-solid and stable network before your deployment begins. Follow standard methods and designs and work with your hardware vendors to make the best possible use of their equipment. Once you plug the thin client in the wall, you will be excited at the things to come and will be ready to configure the application servers.

6
Implementing
the Server

As your project continues, the next step in the process is to design and implement the server that will run all your software. One might be tempted to build and test the thin clients first, but a thin client is not useful until the server is finished and available for testing. As the process unfolds in these pages tips and ideas will be given about how to size the server hardware, how to enable login from thin clients, and how to customize the menus with your own applications.

There are a many distributions of Linux, and two major desktop environments. The desktop provides the software necessary to create the user menus, display the wallpaper, select the color theme, and provide basic file management. One of the major desktops is called KDE and the other is called GNOME. After consideration this chapter will detail the installation of OpenSUSE 10.2 using the GNOME desktop. GNOME has been tested with hundreds of concurrent users in a production environment and many new technologies are available that create an excellent and modern desktop for your users. KDE is excellent as well, and could be deployed in a similar manner.

Planning and Designing the Server

A myriad of hardware options exist and it will be your job to review those choices and make a decision about your deployment. Certain vendors such as IBM, HP, and others are "Linux Friendly". Often Linux distributions are tested on laptops and personal computers, and higher-end hardware might have drivers that are missing or unavailable. One excellent plan is to get a single server from a vendor before you buy all of your computers and load the distribution that you have selected. In recent years driver support in Linux has improved greatly, and the chance of these types of problems has been reduced greatly — but it's still best to keep this in mind.

A number of issues are relevant when selecting hardware. The amount of money in your budget comes into play, as does the total number of users that you will be supporting. Remember that the important number is the concurrent user load versus the total number of users that will be gaining access to the servers. The servers should be placed in a clean, dry location with excellent air conditioning and UPS power. The servers are the lifeline of your deployment and it's important that everything possible is done to provide the most stable environment for them to run.

The part of the server that is most important when running multiple users is the system memory (RAM). Modern CPUs are plenty fast enough for running your software and disk drives are very cheap, and it's very easy to put them into a RAID array. As long as all of your software is able to stay RAM-based and not swap to the disk drives, you will achieve excellent performance. Remember the excellent ability that Linux has — to share memory between processes. Each additional user that runs a software application will run the instance already in memory and only creates a small private workspace for their work files. This allows hundreds of processes to run on one server. If you have not seen multiple users running on Linux or UNIX, and have more of a Microsoft Windows background you will be amazed at how this works. Anecdotal evidence suggests that on the same hardware you can get 2-4 more concurrent users versus the Microsoft Windows platform running centralized applications.

The size of your deployment will offer different challenges. Do some analysis of the number of concurrent people that will be logged into your server and once you have this estimate review the following recommendations.

Up to Fifty Concurrent Users

50 concurrent users would be considered a very small deployment on a Linux server, but would work very well and reliably. A server could be built to run all of the GNOME desktops along with the basic core applications such as Evolution (email), Firefox (browser) and Open Office (word processing). In this case what I call a "Departmental Server" would be deployed and is displayed in the following figure:

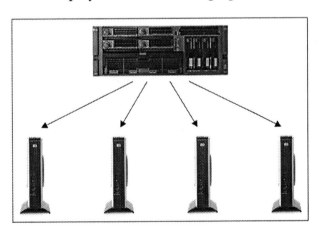

If 99% uptime is good enough for your deployment, this can be achieved by buying a server with RAID disks and redundant hardware such as power supplies. On such servers, in the event of failure the suspect hardware will alert you of a problem and can be swapped out while the server is still running. Obviously, if you have one server there is the potential of some downtime. These types of servers are extremely reliable and provide a very reasonable level of service without the complexity of a cluster.

With that said, if your deployment requires 100% uptime, you will have to consider using a cluster. A second redundant server is installed and the two servers are connected together via software to create one big virtual server. In the event of a failure of one of the servers, the other takes over the running processes and continues to run. This should only be done in situations where downtime is not acceptable. Sometimes, the complexity, cost, and skills required to maintain a cluster offset the very rare occurrences of downtime on a modern computer server. It should also be noted that all servers or hardware need to have redundant devices, or you will still not be able to guarantee 100% uptime.

The estimated hardware to run this type of deployment with GNOME and the core applications would be:

- One Quad CPU Server with Hyper-threading
- 16GB of Memory
- 200GB + of Disk Space

Review your own requirements and make adjustments to these specifications as needed.

Fifty to One Hundred Concurrent Users

As deployments start to get larger, it helps greatly to offload the software applications away from the GNOME desktop. With the GNOME desktop unencumbered with other software, the chance of having to reboot during the day is greatly reduced. With more people and techniques being used, it is rare that the users will cause something that requires a reboot. Rebooting the server running the applications will cause a short disruption of service, but here is the important part—it won't kick them off their thin clients and require them to log in again. If you think back to the "People Issues", one of the things that irritates users is the concept that if the server goes down, everything goes down. This eliminates that issue. It also provides excellent response time and scales very nicely for only a minimal amount of money.

In the following figure, a mid-size deployment is shown. In this design, the GNOME desktop is running on its own server and provides the entryway for the users. From there, as applications are selected from the menu, signals are passed to the second server, and the software applications are activated and remotely displayed back to the thin client. The users cannot tell the difference and are not aware that they are running on 2 physical servers.

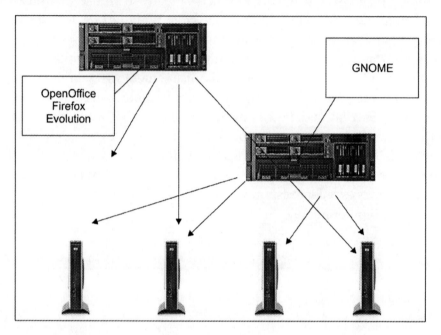

The estimated hardware to run this type of deployment with GNOME and the core applications would be:

- Two Quad CPU Servers with Hyper-threading
- 16GB of Memory on each
- 200GB + of Disk Space on each

Review your own requirements and make adjustments to these specifications as needed. This solution can also be deployed in a cluster, which will require additional hardware.

Over One Hundred Concurrent Users

As deployments get over 100 concurrent users, you will want to explore configuring a server for each of the major applications. This will ensure that the applications have excellent response time and continue to work at speeds that meet your user's expectations. It also provides for easier maintenance on the network and upgrades because only one application at a time is affected. The login server will provide the GNOME desktop and then when applications are launched they will activate the software on the application servers and remotely display it back to the thin client. The users will not be aware that you are running multiple servers in this manner and all will appear to be an integrated desktop. In the figure below, a larger deployment is pictured. Each unique major application gets its own server.

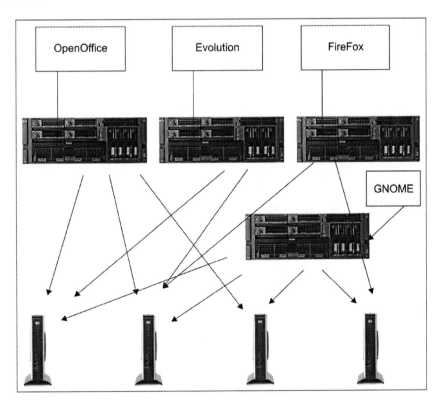

The estimated hardware to run this type of deployment with GNOME and the core applications would be:

- Four Quad CPU Servers with Hyper-threading
- 16GB of Memory on each
- 200GB + of Disk Space on each

Review your own requirements and make adjustments to these specifications as needed. This solution can also be deployed in a cluster, which will require additional hardware.

Customizing for Your Own Deployment

Obviously these diagrams are simplified and designed to show how to scale from a small number of users to hundreds of users. You will have to review the applications that you are going to deploy and then design the specifications based on your needs. You may have packages that you want to continue running in Microsoft Windows instead of some of these Linux applications. They too will run in the same manner from a centralized server.

Building the Server

It is difficult to identify one best Linux distribution to install on the server. There are a lot of variables, which will make certain flavors a better fit for your deployment. One excellent technique is to load several versions of Linux on a standalone computer and review them all before making your choice. Some distributions load better on certain hardware, and offer slightly different software packages that might best fit your need.

The servers will need to be upgraded and should be put in 3 or 4-year rotations. You will save significant dollars by not having to upgrade your thin clients so the cost of purchasing these servers should be easy to absorb. If you are migrating from a client/server deployment, servers would have been required anyway and would have been scheduled for replacement in nearly the same time frame.

Tips on Installing the Operating System

The OpenSUSE 10.2 version of Linux is one of my favorite operating systems because it provides a strong install process, and also incorporates the new gnome-main-menu package, which eliminates the need to run more traditional cascading menus found on KDE and other GNOME desktops.

After picking your distribution, it's time to install. Often during installation, the default disk drive arrangement will not be best suited for a server. Many installs will attempt to split the disk drive into multiple file systems. It is recommended to create two file systems. One has to create the swap device, which should be at least twice the size of the physical memory. The rest of the disk should be used for the / (root) file system and all software will then install into this one directory. The strength of this method is that you will not have the situation where certain file systems fill and require hand tuning. On a server that needs to be up for thin client deployments, the fewer things that need to be maintained the better. Another viewpoint is that it's best to allow the operating system to install into multiple disk volume, which perhaps might better isolate you from circumstances such as the users filling a drive and causing problems with the underlying operating system.

Appendix B contains step-by-step instructions for installing OpenSUSE 10.2 and activating a basic server capable of supporting thin clients. Other flavors of Linux would have very similar steps. Because of the diversity of these steps, it was not placed in this chapter.

Once installed, very little tuning or changes will be required. Unlike older Intel versions of UNIX, Linux works well for hundreds of users immediately. If the server you have purchased has a large amount of memory, make sure that the operating system is seeing all of the memory. Some distributions have a 'bigmem' kernel that might need to be installed by hand. Running the 'top' command from a terminal window will show you the amount of memory the operating system is seeing.

Enabling XDMCP

There are multiple methods to allow the thin clients to connect to the server. Solutions such as VNC, NoMachine, and Metaframe for UNIX can be deployed and each has its pros and cons. VNC for instance is normally not used for regular user sessions, but might provide you with the best possible connection method to certain operating systems such as Mac OS X. When regular network speeds are available, using native X-windows is recommended. This license-free transport provides an excellent, crisp, and responsive method to run remotely displayed applications. For the sake of simplicity and concept, the XDMCP method of login is used in these pages.

Creating a Custom Login Screen

If you remember back to the "People Issues", sometimes presentation and minor details are as important as the technical design. It is recommended therefore that the first step in this process is to design a custom login screen that will be displayed during the authentication process. This is immediately noticed by users, and should be one of the first things that you show them. This along with a wide selection of wallpapers and quality icons will give them a 'wow' factor that will greatly help the transition.

Fortunately, it's very easy to create your own login screen. The steps will be similar in the various distributions, though these instructions are for OpenSUSE 10.2.

1. The login themes are loaded dynamically and are stored in `/opt/gnome/share/gdm/themes`.

2. Once in that directory create a new directory and call it something that relates to your logo design.

3. Now go into another theme and copy the contents of that directory into your new directory as a template. Each of the default themes has a file called `screenshot.png`, which shows you what that theme looks like. Use that to pick one that is close to your desired final login screen.

4. Now, go back into your custom theme directory and change the file `background.svg` to match the desired colors that best suit your needs.

As an example, lets say that Packt Publishing required a login screen with its company colors, which are orange, black, white, and gray. The following steps show you how to alter the image as desired:

1. The file `background.svg` should be opened with a program that supports editing SVG images such as Inkscape. In the next figure, the default background, which is blue, is opened and ready for editing:

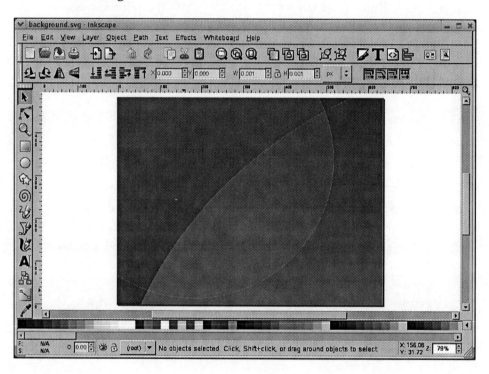

2. Using the Inkscape interface change the colors of the background to match the colors desired. Once completed your background will look similar to the following screenshot. Save the new SVG image.

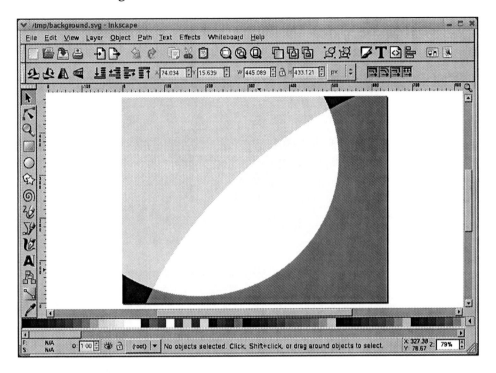

3. In your custom directory the file GdmGreeterTheme.desktop
    contains the information relevant to the design of the theme.
    Change the contents of that file and fill in the Greeter, Name,
    Description, Author, Copyright, and Screenshot fields. Often, this
    file has been internationalized and the entries that you do not
    need can be deleted. The finished example is displayed
    as follows:

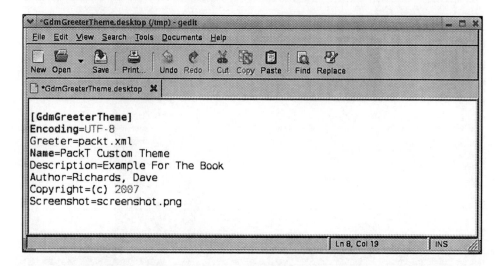

4. In the theme that you copied there is a .xml file. Rename this file
    to match what appears on the **Greeter=** line in the file you just
    edited. Many of the themes contain a logo or graphical image in
    the lower right-hand corner of the screen. Overwrite that image in
    your custom theme directory with your own corporate or desired
    logo. At this point you have a working theme that is available
    for use. Make sure that you test the login theme at the various
    resolutions such as 800x600, 1024x768, 1280x1024, and so on,
    and verify that it displays correctly.

The completed example as it appears to connecting thin clients is pictured in the following figure:

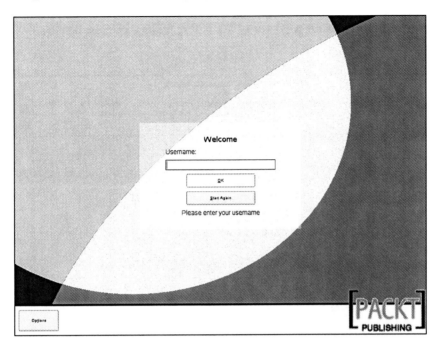

Creating a Custom Splash Page

Further customization can be obtained by changing the default splash that appears when GNOME is activated. This appears for a few seconds at the beginning of the session. This image is in PNG format and is in the directory `/opt/gnome/share/dist/splash` with a file name `dist-splash.png`. Always backup the old image before editing. These minor touches will help in impressing management and the user community.

Using a graphical editor such as GIMP, create a new image that is 450x285 pixels. Use the colors and logo of your organization to continue to present your users with a comfortable look and feel.

The figure below shows a custom PACKT splash page that could be deployed.

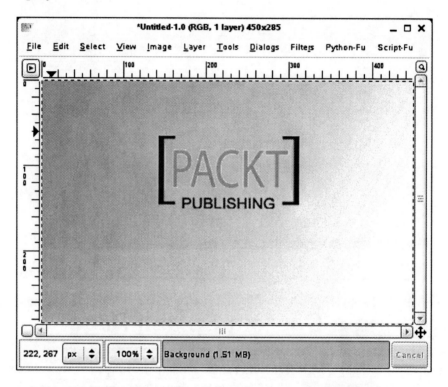

Enable Login Screen and XDMCP with gdmsetup

You are now ready to enable XDMCP logins from your thin clients. This is easily handled with the program gdmsetup. Invoke the gdmsetup command. The important settings are in the **Local**, **Remote**, and **Security** tabs.

The **Local** tab screen of gdmsetup appears as follows:

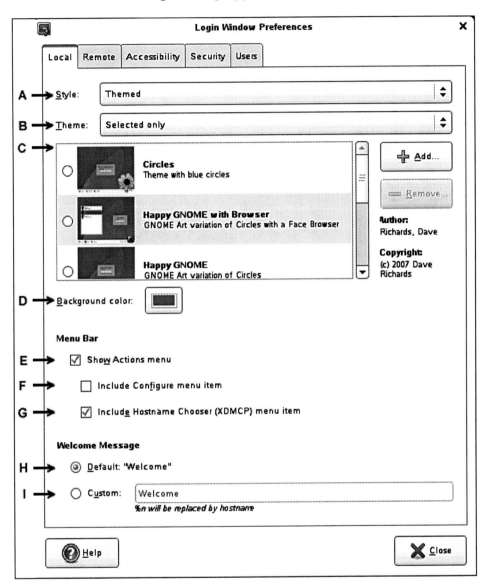

The chart below describes the lettered items from the tabs mentioned above.

Tab	Letter	Description
Local		
	A	The style of login screen to display on the system console.
		Plain: A plain login screen with selectable color
		Plain with face browser: A plain login screen with a user name chooser list.
		Themed: A more complex, pre-designed wallpaper.
		Select **Themed** to display the graphical login.
	B	The theme type for the system console.
		Selected only:
		Use only one that you have selected.
		Random from selected:
		Randomly use several themes you have selected.
		Select **Selected only** to force the choice you have selected to be used for all users.
	C	Select the theme that you would like to use.
		This is where you would select the customized theme that you created, or use one of the default themes. Make sure that you depress the radio button to the left of the desired theme.
	D	Configure the Background color. This color will be used on transparent sections of the theme.
		Unless you have a transparent layer, this won't be seen.
	E	Configure whether to Show Actions menu bar or not. The actions menu optionally appears on the login screen to give the users additional options.
		Uncheck this option to reduce the amount of actions available on the login screen. You probably will want to disable this feature

Tab	Letter	Description
Local		
	F	Toggle whether to add the Configure menu on the menu bar. This adds additional options on the console.
		This item will not be selectable when option E is disabled.
	G	The XDMCP Chooser option. This allows the console to generate an XDMCP chooser of all available servers allowing this type of connection.
		This item will not be selectable when option E is disabled.
	H	The Default **Welcome** option toggles whether to display a generic fixed message on the console
		This item will not be selectable when option I is disabled.
	I	The Custom login message is configured here. You can type in the name of your company or any message you desire.
		Check this option and customize to make the login screen more presentable for your users.

The **Remote** tab screen of gdmsetup appears as follows:

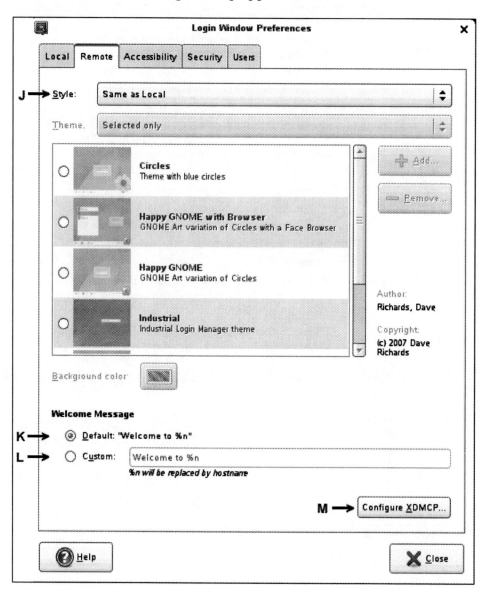

Tab	Letter	Description
Remote		
	J	The login screen style to use for all remote XDMCP connections.
		Remote login disabled: Users cannot log in remotely, and only the system console allows logins.
		Same as Local: The settings configured for the system console are replicated for remote XDMCP users.
		Plain: A plain login is presented.
		Plain with face browser: A plain login is presented, along with a chooser of system users.
		Select **Same as Local** to display the graphical login.
	K	The Default **Welcome** option toggles whether to display a generic fixed message on the console
		This item will not be selectable when option I is disabled.
	L	The Custom login message is configured here. You can type in the name of your company or any message you desire.
		Check this option and customize to make the login screen more presentable for your users.
	M	Configure XDMCP allows you to further tune remote requests to the server. The settings will allow you to define the total number of connections, and tune the server to avoid being overloaded.

The **Security** tab screen of gdmsetup appears as follows:

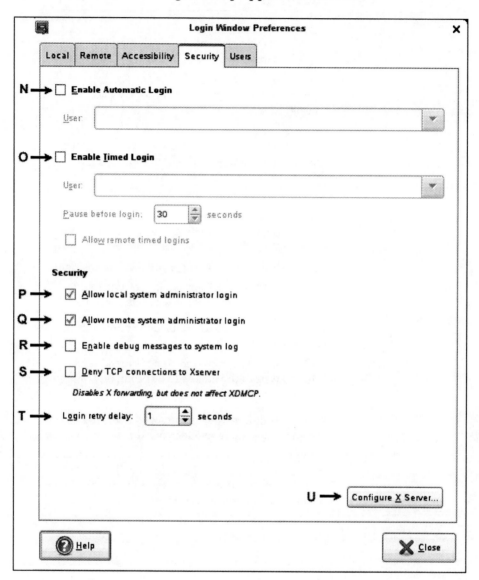

Tab	Letter	Description
Security		
	N	Toggles whether to enable automatic login on the system console to a particular user. This is only used for standalone personal computers that do not require user accounts. This option should be disabled.
	O	Toggles whether to enable a timed automatic login on the system console. This is only used for standalone personal computers that do not require user accounts. This option should be disabled.
	P	Toggle whether the 'root' account can log into the system console. Allow this based on your security requirements.
	Q	Toggle whether the 'root' account can log into the XDMCP authentication system. Allow this based on your security requirements. Normally, 'root' graphical login from remote terminals is disabled.
	R	Toggle whether to enable debug messages to the system log. This will increase the level of detail the server keeps in regards to X and login activities. This feature might be useful to troubleshoot problems, but normally isn't required.
	S	Toggle whether or not to deny TCP connections to the X-server. This is used as a security feature.
	T	Allows you to configure the amount of time to wait after failed password before the prompt is redisplayed. This is used for security reasons.
	U	Allows you to configure the X server of the system console. This allows you to fine-tune the behavior of the server. Normally this will not be changed.

Option "J" is the setting that will enable XDMCP logins. Once configured, thin clients will be able to connect and log into the server. With these few steps you have created a custom login and granted permissions for the thin clients to begin using the server. XDMCP was used for the sake of simplicity and as a demonstration of desktop logins. You will need to review your security requirements and possibly will deploy a secure shell for X-windows connections if required.

Authentication Methods

Several different methods for password management are available on Linux servers. The simplest method is to just use passwords found on the server itself. Scripts can be developed to propagate passwords to any back-up or redundant servers that are also used for login purposes. Remember that if you set up servers to offload certain applications from the primary desktop, then the user will never physically log into those servers in a manner that requires password and they don't have to be assigned. Another method available to Linux servers is the ability to use LDAP for passwords. The servers would then authenticate against this database and instantly sync passwords between all servers.

Providing the Desktop

Though KDE and GNOME both provide excellent solutions that will work perfectly well on thin clients, we shall choose GNOME for our example and discuss it in greater detail.

Modern distributions with GNOME provide a strong selection of applications immediately upon installation all with menus fully installed. In smaller deployments, the servers might be ready for use after enabling the XDMCP protocol. In OpenSUSE 10.2, Firefox, Evolution, and OpenOffice.org are supported and installed with GNOME.

Using the Main Menu

Traditional cascading menus are not effective. The new Main Menu module (otherwise known as the **slab**) has been merged into the new version of OpenSUSE. When the user clicks on the "**Computer**" icon on the lower panel, a pop-up window opens and displays the most commonly used applications. For most people, a group of 6 or 8 applications is all they will ever need and this new design makes it easy for them to navigate. The following figure shows the new main menu as featured in GNOME.

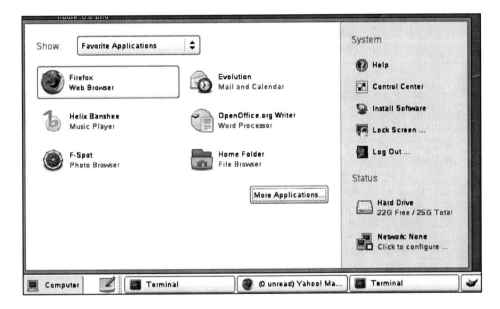

As you can see from the image, one click provides nearly everything that a typical user would ever want to use on the desktop. However, if they need to access other applications, clicking on **More Applications...** will present the rest of the software for their use.

The next figure shows the More Applications screen.

The following table shows the locations of the files that are edited to change the appearance of the application browser. Make sure that backups are made of files and directories before you attempt to make custom changes. That will allow you to restore items as required as they are altered. These directories are on OpenSUSE 10.2, while other distributions will be similar. Tools exist to make these changes graphically, but the files are being shown to ensure that enough documentation exists for you to proceed.

Directory	File Name	Description
`/opt/xdg/menus`	`applications.menu`	This is where the Groups found in the figure opposite are added, deleted or edited.
`/usr/share/ desktop-directories`	`*.directory`	The descriptions of the groups are stored here. This is the string that displays for each group in multiple languages.
`/usr/share/pixmaps`	`*.png`	Icons that are available for use next to the names of each software application.
`/opt/gnome/share/ pixmaps`	`*.png`	Icons that are available for use next to the names of each software application.
`/usr/share/ applications`	`*.desktop`	The software applications are enabled and placed into Groups in this directory.
`/opt/gnome/share/ applications`	`*.desktop`	The software applications are enabled and placed into Groups in this directory.

Creating Custom Program Icons

All of the applications that you install from the distribution will automatically add and delete the `.desktop` files and appropriately update the Main Menu. There will be circumstances where you will want to add your own icons. The `.desktop` files are easy to create by hand. The best method is to duplicate a file for a similar application and then edit it by hand. If you are going to start creating your own applications and scripts, it is recommended to create the directories as seen in the following table. Having them away from `/usr/bin` or `/usr/local/ bin` will allow for easy backups and migration to other servers without backing up binaries already in those directories.

Directory	Purpose
/u2/local/bin	Custom Scripts
/u2/local/lib	Custom libraries and items accessed by your custom scripts
/u2/local/skel	Default settings that are loaded into user directories

It is also recommended that all .desktop files run a shell script instead of calling the program itself. The reason for this is because sometimes users will link and pull out icons to their desktop or panel, and once this is done, it creates a copy of that file and will not pick up your most recent changes. If you call a shell script, changes made are always picked up by the users.

The figure below shows a custom .desktop file being created. The .desktop file for Mozilla Firefox was copied and then altered. This was found in the Internet group and therefore the custom application appears there as well.

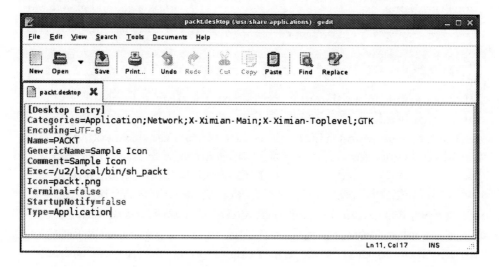

In the table below each of the lines in the figure are described:

Line Type	Description
Categories	The Group/Categories under which this item should display on the Main Menu
Name	The application name that should appear on the main menu
GenericName	The secondary description line that appears below the application name on the main menu
Comment	A longer description of this application
Exec	The program or shell script to execute when this icon is clicked
Icon	The file name of the icon to appear next to the name of the application
Terminal	If this Icon requires a terminal window to run
StartupNotify	Whether or not to have feedback on the mouse when the application has been clicked
Type	The type of application

Once this file is saved, a new icon immediately displays for all users in the main menu and is ready for use. Users do not have to log off and back on to the server to pick up these changes. This feature allows you to make instant changes for hundreds of users at a time without having to touch their desktops.

In the following figure the new sample application has been added as PACKT.

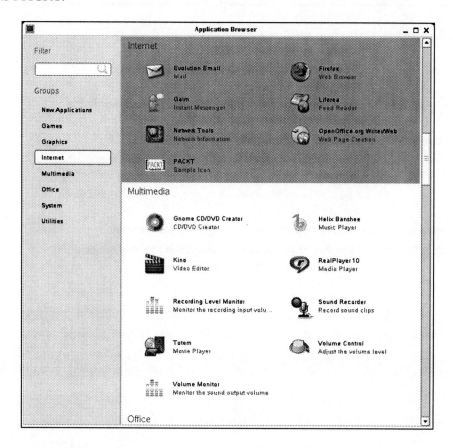

Once the icon is visible, if the user clicks on the new **PACKT** icon, it will attempt to run /u2/local/bin/sh_packt as was specified in the Exec command.

Writing Custom Graphical Dialogs

As you are developing scripts and adding custom icons, you may be required to query the user with questions. On a graphical desktop, you will not want a text-based prompt to come open and display. The program Zenity is an excellent tool that allows you to integrate graphical dialogs with command-line scripts. They also require no compiling or development and are very easy to build and migrate easily in operating system upgrades.

Zenity offers an extensive number of command-line arguments, and this example will tell you how to invoke the dialog and take action with a script. The following figure shows a small script that invokes a prompt and then when the user selects a button, it drops through and can perform any steps that you wish.

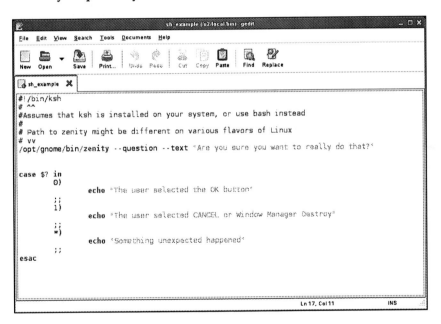

When this command is run, a dialog will appear as shown in the next figure.

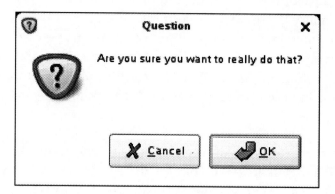

The case statement in the shell script receives the response and then allows you to decide what steps to perform. In this case a zero (0) is returned if the user selects **OK** and one (1) is returned if the **CANCEL** or **X** in the window manager is selected.

Adding Custom Scripts before GNOME Starts

When the distributions are engineered, they are tested with the understanding that users will be running on a stand alone computer or laptop. So sometimes you will have to install some additional scripts that are invoked before the GNOME desktop starts. On OpenSUSE 10.2 the file that is run after authentication is
`/etc/opt/gnome/gdm/Xsession`, immediately before the
`exec /etc/X11/xdm/Xsession $1 $GDM_LANG` where custom changes can be installed. It is advisable to perform the following things before GNOME is activated:

- Verify that the user is not already logged in and if they are give them a zenity prompt asking if they want to terminate their other session. There are two situations where this will happen: one when the user left their session logged in at their desk and is attempting to log in from another location, and second when the user did not log off correctly and left processes on the server. Often, users will simply turn off their thin clients without first logging out, and sometimes processes are not terminated correctly.

- Poll the process list and terminate any stray processes they have left running. Sometimes a few of the processes get stuck and are left behind, even when they log out correctly. This will ensure that a fresh clean set of daemons are started with each login.

- Insert or update `gconf` settings that you want to force into their session. Sometimes users will stumble into settings that cause problems in the various applications, and when you identify some you can force them back to reasonable defaults before GNOME is activated again.

- Some bandwidth management applications for sending X-windows over slower speeds are greatly slowed by complex wallpapers. Scripts can be written to detect login method and if users are logging in over low bandwidth alter their wallpaper back to a solid color.

Enabling 3D Desktop Support

Quite recently technology has become available on the Linux desktops that make use of more advanced features of video cards. Two session managers, Compiz and Beryl provide features such as a 3-dimensional desktop, shadowing, and transparencies. Thin clients can be built with either ATI or Nvidia video cards and the effects will remotely display over the network at very acceptable speeds. Tests on a Gigabit network, with 100 Megabit to the desktop indicate that all resolutions in 16 bit color are responsive, and 24-bit color works in 1024x768. The limiting factor was the network itself, and it's very likely that additional gains could be achieved with Gigabit to the desktop. If you are considering deploying this technology, do some testing of your own and verify that the plugins and features that you require are working over your own network.

The method for invoking the 3-dimensional desktop is pretty straight-forward. During the login process the server should verify whether the user has requested this type of display and then verify that the hardware they are using supports advanced video.

The next figure shows what can be achieved with Beryl remote displayed to a thin client.

NFS Mounts and Shared Directories

On a smaller deployment, disk space will not be an issue. But as more and more users are writing files it might help your deployment to install a small server just to handle disk storage. It is possible to successfully deploy a server that has the sole purpose of providing disk space for hundreds of concurrent users. The disk space server can be loaded with Linux and then NFS mounted to the rest of the servers on your network. Files that are written over NFS retain the permissions of the owner and group of the files. The advantage of this design is that file backups and restorations can be performed without using the bus or controllers of your servers running software processes. Some backup and restoration software packages are a bit CPU intensive, and with this design, the users will not be slowed while this is being performed. Another advantage of offloading the disk activity to its own server is that sometimes backup software will require a different flavor of Linux than you want to deploy on your primary server, and this provides the flexibility of mixing and matching distributions very easily.

Integrating Bandwidth Management for Remote Users

As you fine-tune the thin clients you are going to purchase, most likely a part of your deployment will be on a device that runs on low bandwidth. Solutions such as VNC or NoMachine might be good solutions for you. Another fit might be to purchase and use Citrix Metaframe for UNIX. Its main advantage is the plethora of devices that it supports including computers of various operating systems, handheld operating systems, and cell phones. This is a licensed product and will garner some additional costs. One issue that is faced with this product is that it doesn't run on the Linux operating system. This is unfortunate, but a solution presents itself should this be the right fit for you. Citrix Metaframe for

UNIX supports Solaris Sparc. The users on low bandwidth log into the Solaris server, and an X-windows session is initiated and then a remote-shell or secure-shell command can be passed to your Linux GNOME server, invoking a full session exactly as is seen on desktop thin clients. The beauty of this design is that this creates a true roaming desktop. A user can move from desktop thin client, to remote wireless laptop, to cell phone, and all of their software applications and work files go with them.

Summary

The server design requires much thought and analysis. It's the most important part of the solution and a good design will offer a very stable environment for your organization. It's best to keep things flexible and easy to change and maintain, and centralized servers will provide that very well. The user community will find little things that were missed during testing, and each time that happens it's an opportunity to improve the system. The server is now up and running, and now it's time to become familiar with the software.

7

Implementing the User Software

This next chapter is about *ideas*. Often, individuals that are considering Linux deployments do not really even know where to start. Thin clients and Linux servers work extremely well; however, if software is not found to meet your users' needs, they are worthless. Small organizations might be able to deploy a 100% Linux solution while larger deployments probably will have a mixture of multiple operating systems including Microsoft Windows. Often, the core packages and 80% or higher of what is required for day-to-day use can be run on Linux without costly licenses.

Running Software from a Remote Server

In the previous chapter it was mentioned that multiple servers can be used to scale software applications in larger deployments. Depending on your needs, applications like **rsh** (Remote Shell) and **ssh** (Secure Shell) can be used to pass a 'bundle' from the primary GNOME server to the application servers. For the sake of simplicity, the use of rsh is conceptually described.

The following figure shows the basic functionality of offloading software applications to other servers. The user clicks on an icon on the GNOME desktop and instead of running that particular application on the same computer, it's instead offloaded to a second server. The user is not aware that their session has been passed on to other physical hardware.

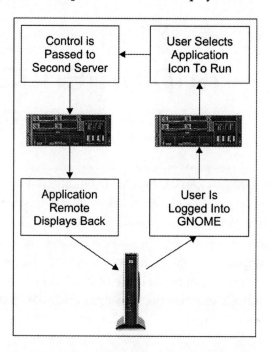

Experimenting with this concept requires that rsh and rsh-server should be installed on two computers. A review of the rsh main page indicates that two properties are required for an rsh to work correctly: the user must be present on the second computer and also a file called .rhosts must be in their home directory. The rhosts file controls which servers should be able to gain access to the rsh remote server. Make sure to always configure users on multiple machines with the same group and user-ID numbers, to avoid file protection problems. Also, keep in mind that it is possible that a user will never gain access to the application servers via a login, so you can set all of their passwords to hardened passwords — they aren't ever used. Login only occurs on the GNOME primary servers.

If you are logged into the GNOME primary server as a user and want to test this concept, run the following command:

```
rsh <second_computer> date
```

Here `<second_computer>` is the name of the application server. If **Permission denied** appears, then either the account is not on the second server, or the `.rhosts` file is not configured correctly. The date that was physically performed on the application server should return on the command line. When invoking larger applications such as Firefox in this manner, you will want to create scripts on the remote server. Often, there are environmental variables and command-line functions that need to be performed before the binary is started. You also will probably have to pass `$DISPLAY` on the command line and set it on the remote server in the shell. The
start-up scripts should also terminate any running occurrences of the same software package. Users will often forget that a software package is running already, and launch the same program again. They also will sometimes lock up the software, and can easily be trained to just re-launch the program to fully terminate any stuck sessions.

The ssh (Secure Shell) can be used in the same manner if required and performs the same steps as the rsh, except the fact that it's encrypted.

Planning which User Software to Deploy

Once again it should be mentioned that your primary focus should be the more commodity-type software that is easier to deploy on Linux. Specialized applications that you already have running on Microsoft Windows can be left there for the initial rollout and then reviewed later. A deployment of thin clients, new servers, and new software will be a major project in itself, and is the best area of focus in the first pass.

Many applications are available on Linux to meet the basic needs of electronic mail, word processing, internet surfing, picture processing, and audio/video playback. The applications on these pages work very well in the GNOME desktop. If your deployment will be in KDE, applications of equal quality are available.

In the following pages, we will be reviewing software applications to be considered as part of your deployment. At the end of each section is a table, which reviews the application. Two categories appear: one being "Thin Client Performance" and the other being "Multi-User Performance". These observations are based on years of experience in a deployment with hundreds of users. Further descriptions of these categories follow:

Thin Client Performance

Excellent	This application runs equally well on the system console and over remote display to thin clients. There is no difference in speed or features.
Very Good	This application runs very well on thin clients, but is slightly slower than on the system console. These applications are perfectly suited for deployment and the speed difference is minimal.

Multi-User Performance

Excellent	This program has a small memory footprint and makes good use of shared memory. Hundreds of concurrent instances of this application can be achieved easily.
Very Good	This program makes good use of shared memory, but consumes more memory. The server you deploy will need to have more memory to achieve the results that you desire.

It's now time to offer suggestions of applications that work well on thin clients and fit nicely into the GNOME desktop.

Browser

A web browser is a critical piece of a modern computer. Users will need to gain access to not only internal web-based applications, but a plethora of functionality via the Internet.

Firefox

The Firefox browser has become very popular in recent years, and it's entirely possible you have already used this program. Functionality is nearly identical on Linux, Microsoft Windows, and Mac OS X. When installing on multi-user Linux, one copy is installed and everyone runs the same version. Global plugins are made available from that common install directory. Users are able to add their own add-ons which are installed into their private home directory.

As part of your testing, make sure that all sites that your users will need to visit render correctly with Firefox. Sloppy and poorly written sites are still out there, and not all web developers test with browsers besides Internet Explorer. In recent years, this issue has gotten much better. Make sure that you test Firefox on Linux if that is your target platform. Some sites work correctly on Firefox for Microsoft Windows, but not for the versions of Linux and Mac. If there are a few sites that will just not work in Firefox, then this isn't a failure and certainly shouldn't halt deployment. Simply configure a session of Internet Explorer for those few people that need to gain access to those sites and everyone else can run Firefox. Pressure the developers of such content to do the right thing and make it platform neutral.

The next figure shows Firefox running on the Linux platform.

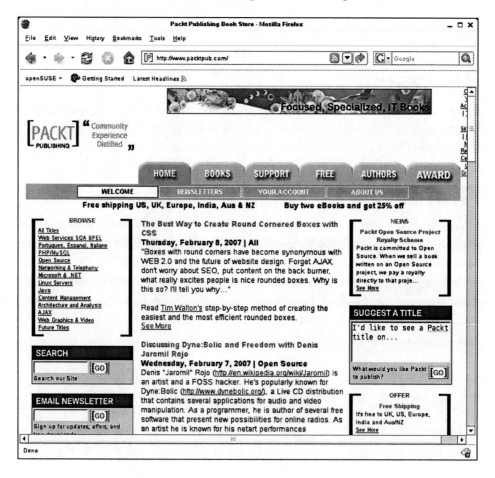

Software Application	Firefox 2.0
License	MPL/GPL/LGPL
Thin Client Performance	Very Good
Multi-User Performance	Very Good
Operating Systems	Win32, Linux, Mac OS X

Electronic Mail

Users in nearly all job duties will need to gain access to electronic mail. Modern email clients also need to provide calendaring, task, memo, and address book capabilities.

Evolution

The Evolution software package is an excellent tool to provide electronic mail, contacts, calendars, memos, and tasks. With enough server memory, Evolution scales to hundreds of concurrent users. It can use free transports for message delivery such as Sendmail, or connect to more a robust back end such as Groupwise or Exchange.

The following figure shows Evolution email:

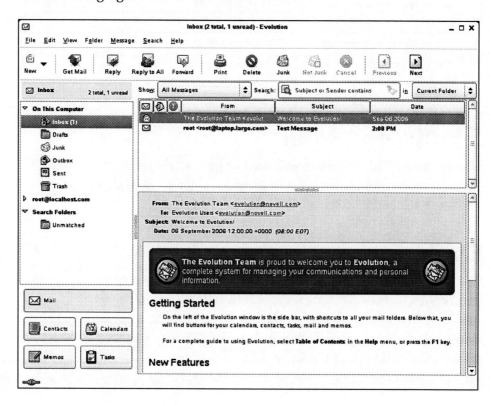

The contacts tool provided by the Evolution software is shown in the following figure:

The next three figures show the Evolution calendar, Evolution memos, and Evolution tasks respectively.

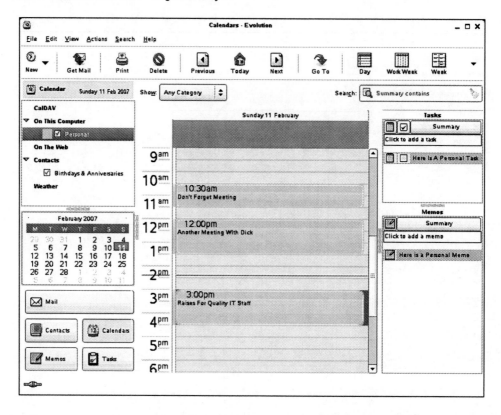

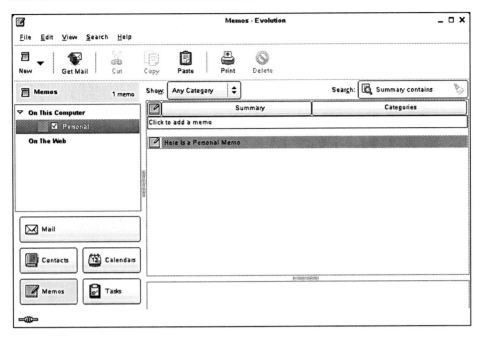

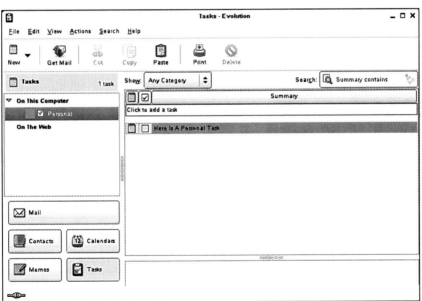

Software Application	Evolution
License	GPL
Thin Client Performance	Excellent
Multi-User Performance	Very Good
Operating Systems	Win32, Linux, Mac OS X

Mail Notification

Mail notification is a very useful panel applet that alerts you of any new messages that are received. It works with most post office back ends and presents a popup when new messages arrive. This minor application is welcomed by users.

The next figure shows a mail-notification window alerting the user of a new message.

Software Application	Mail Notification
License	GPL
Thin Client Performance	Excellent
Multi-User Performance	Excellent
Operating Systems	Linux

Office Suite

At some point of time, nearly all users will need to create documents or spreadsheets. There are some excellent stand-alone packages that recreate much of this functionality. I am of the opinion that it's best to have an integrated suite. This will provide a consistent interface, and easier sharing of information and data.

OpenOffice.org

The OpenOffice.org productivity suite provides the following modules:

- **Writer** — Word Processing (Similar to Microsoft Word)
- **Calc** — Spreadsheet (Similar to Microsoft Excel)
- **Impress** — Presentation (Similar to Microsoft Powerpoint)
- **BASE** — Data Base (Similar to Microsoft Access)
- **Draw** — Frame Based Documents

With enough memory, hundreds of concurrent OpenOffice.org sessions can be run on one server. The installation is placed in one directory which is shared by all users. Custom user settings are stored in the home directory for each person. When run from one server, all users are always on the same version and share the same fonts, which provide a very stable working environment and reduces support calls.

The various modules of OpenOffice.org running on Linux are shown in the following figure:

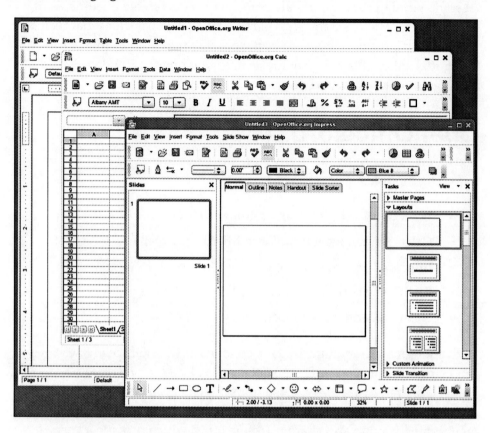

Software Application	OpenOffice.org
License	GPL
Thin Client Performance	Very Good
Multi-User Performance	Very Good
Operating Systems	Win32, Linux, Mac OS X, Solaris

Tomboy

Tomboy is an excellent Wiki style note-taking application. Instead of taking notes in the manner a developer has already created, Tomboy has no boundaries and allows almost endless possibilities. Once launched, Tomboy will sit on the gnome panel as an icon. When designing a multi-server environment, it's best to run Tomboy on the same computer as Evolution to allow linking between these two products. The next figure shows Tomboy running and two notes that have been linked together.

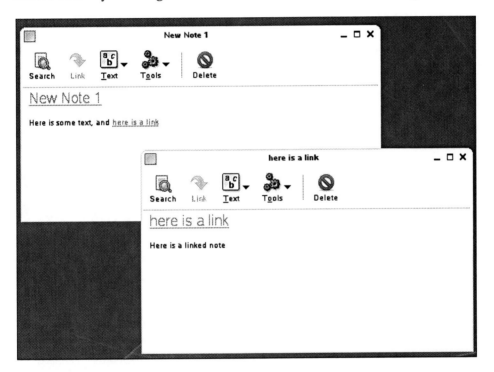

Software Application	Tomboy
License	GPL
Thin Client Performance	Excellent
Multi-User Performance	Excellent
Operating Systems	Linux

Planner

Planner is a simple time-management application that might be useful for your projects. While not as robust as products on other operating systems, the basic functionality is provided. Work is developing in the area of integration with Evolution. The screenshot below is a shot of Planner running on Linux (Planner Project Management System).

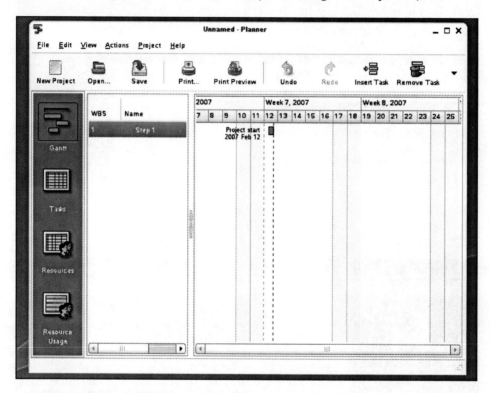

Software Application	Planner
License	GPL
Thin Client Performance	Excellent
Multi-User Performance	Excellent
Operating Systems	Linux

Instant Messaging

A great deal of communication is done via instant messages. If appropriate for your organization, messages can be sent to the various instant messaging networks right from the Linux desktop.

Pidgin

Pidgin is used for your instant messaging needs. Pidgin will connect you to a myriad of back ends including Yahoo, MSN, AOL, and ICQ. It can also be used on an intranet using the Jabber protocol. Jabber is open source and can be installed on a server to provide communication between your users without having to allow them access to the Internet.

The following figure shows Pidgin running and using the Jabber protocol.

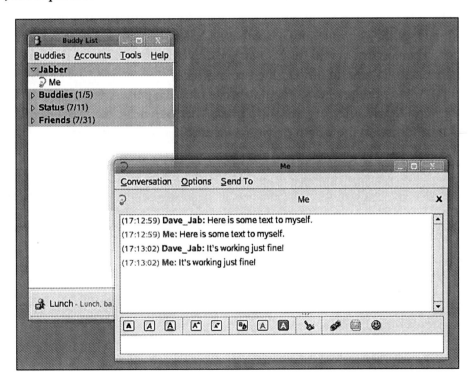

Software Application	GAIM
License	GPL
Thin Client Performance	Excellent
Multi-User Performance	Excellent
Operating Systems	Win32, Linux

File Processing

As more and more files are placed on your network, it becomes important to provide tools for searches. While searching for file names was appropriate in years past, it's now common to data-mine the text of all documents.

Beagle

Beagle is an indexing system that searches your documents and files, and indexes the contents into a database. On smaller servers with fewer users, it can be run in real time. In larger deployments, it can be done in batch mode via **cron** to offload the processing of documents to night-time hours. A wide range of document formats including those from Microsoft Office and OpenOffice.org are supported. The user run-time processes can be attached to their own private data and shared directories.

The following figure shows the Beagle search query application and information being returned.

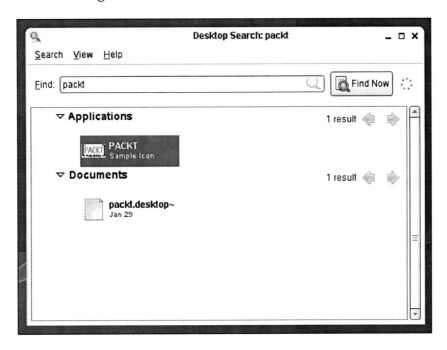

Software Application	Beagle
License	GPL
Thin Client Performance	Excellent
Multi-User Performance	Excellent
Operating Systems	Linux

Picture Processing

Digital images and clipart are commonly used in nearly all aspects of the computer environment. Very often the pictures require modification before they can be used for their final functionality. It's important to provide the capability to users to alter pictures in order to suit their needs.

GIMP

GIMP is a picture editor. It allows you to create, alter, and resize images, and write them in the common image formats. It runs well on thin clients and provides a great solution for users that need to make adjustments to pictures. The next figure shows the GIMP software application running on Linux.

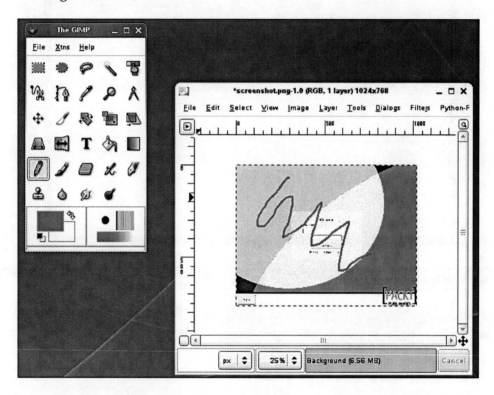

Software Application	GIMP
License	GPL
Thin Client Performance	Very Good
Multi-User Performance	Excellent
Operating Systems	Win32, Linux, Mac OS X

F-Spot

F-Spot is a photo-management package. It imports files, saves them into
an archive, and allows them to be easily managed. For users that are
taking lots of digital photos, this is an excellent package for them to use.
The next figure shows F-Spot running on the Linux platform.

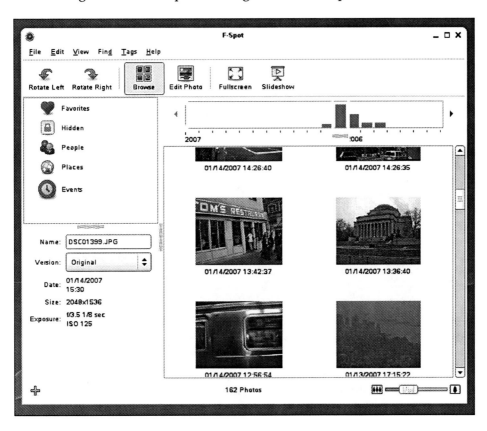

Software Application	F-Spot
License	GPL
Thin Client Performance	Excellent
Multi-User Performance	Excellent
Operating Systems	Linux

Audio and Video Processing

Audio and video files are commonly used for various reasons. You will have to review the needs of your organization, and then provide the appropriate software to hear and view those files.

Xine

The Xine library and UI will allow you to play many types of video and audio formats to the thin clients. In the following figure it's playing a CD with the default skin.

Software Application	Xine
License	GPL
Thin Client Performance	Very Good
Multi-User Performance	Excellent
Operating Systems	Linux

Real Player

The Real Player can be used as well to play back video feeds. Depending on your needs, this might provide a better fit than Xine. This application is also widely used on Microsoft Windows and your users might already be familiar with its use.

The next figure shows the Real Player application running.

Software Application	Real Player
License	GPL
Thin Client Performance	Very Good
Multi-User Performance	Excellent
Operating Systems	Win32, Linux, Mac OS X

Databases

While licensed products such as Oracle will run on Linux, in many cases you will be able to deploy applications with open-source databases. In doing so, major dollars can be saved in licensing costs.

MySQL

The MySQL database can be used to store your data for web-based applications and also more traditional graphic packages that you develop. OpenOffice.org can also directly query MySQL databases and import data directly into the various modules.

Software Application	MySQL
License	MPL/GPL/LGPL
Thin Client Performance	NA
Multi-User Performance	NA
Operating Systems	Linux

PostgreSQL

PostgreSQL provides a data store in the same way as MySQL. After reviewing your development and run-time needs, this might be a better fit should your software be developed around this database.

Software Application	PostgreSQL
License	
Thin Client Performance	NA
Multi-User Performance	NA
Operating Systems	Linux

Software Development

There are various software frameworks that are used to develop and run various types of applications.

Mono

Mono is used to develop and run .NET applications. Graphical applications developed in this manner fit nicely into the GNOME desktop, and provide a very clean-looking desktop environment. The Tomboy and Beagle applications are developed using Mono.

Software Application	Mono
License	GPL
Thin Client Performance	Excellent
Multi-User Performance	Very Good
Operating Systems	Linux

Connection to Legacy UNIX Servers

There are still a high number of applications developed to run in character mode on UNIX or Linux servers. Robust applications that emulate either ANSI or VT100 style terminals are available in the form of two applications:

gnome-terminal

This application fits very nicely into the GNOME environment and is complete for many deployments, though feedbacks at times still indicate that it has slower performance than users' expectations. So test this in your environment and verify its speed. If it works fine, it provides a much nicer-looking interface than xterm.

xterm

An oldie but goodie, xterm is feature rich via the command line, and offers blazingly fast performance even on remote display. Emulation is excellent and can be customized greatly. It lacks some UI polish, but your users might very well appreciate the better performance.

Connection to Legacy IBM Mainframes

Many applications still run on IBM Mainfames, and require 3270 or similar emulation. The software package X3270 can be used to gain access to these types of computers. Like xterm, X3270 is robust and allows a great deal of customization.

The following figure shows X3270 running on the Linux platform

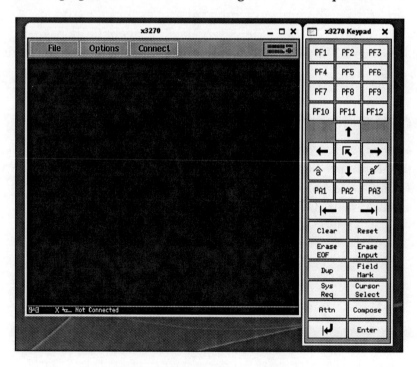

Connection to Microsoft Windows Applications

If you already have a centralized Microsoft Windows deployed with Citrix, then a Citrix client is available for Linux and can be deployed. The Linux client will integrate nicely into your desktop and will run concurrently with your deployed Linux packages. The client supports a high number of command-line flags, which allow you to customize the user experience.

If you wish to run applications via RDP, the Rdesktop application is available. This excellent open-source project allows you to form a connection to the Windows servers and run applications just as you would from a personal computer. The Rdesktop commands are connected to icons in the GNOME desktop. When a user clicks on the icon, the Microsoft Windows applications will open and display on the thin client.

In the following figure, a terminal window has invoked a Rdesktop session and is running Paint.

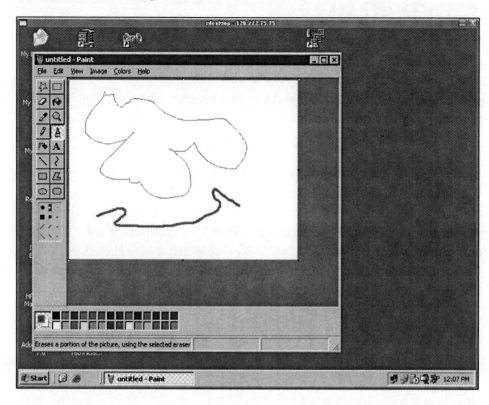

Summary

All of the applications in this chapter should be reviewed and tested within your environment to ensure that they are a good fit for your organization. All have been tested in a production environment and should provide the same functionality that your users are already accessing with their personal computers. With testing, correct deployment, and training, you will soon be offering a cost-free set of core applications and begin to save money.

We now have built your servers and found software applications to run on Linux. It's time now to build your thin clients.

8

Implementing the Thin Clients

The beauty of using thin clients is that all of the work in the previous chapters has gotten you virtually to completion of your project. Unlike a traditional personal computer network where the desktop is the start, in this type of deployment, the desktop is the end. You have been able to simulate the user experience from the console of the server itself, and now are simply providing the monitor, mouse, keyboard, and desktops to allow users to gain access to the software.

Choosing the Right Thin Client

As you review thin client hardware the following considerations should be made:

Money

The amount of money in your budget will impact your thin clients. Even if you have explained the duty cycle of these devices, you still must weigh a return on investment. Thin clients for desktops are priced starting around 200 dollars and go up to about 700 dollars. The higher-end devices will give you faster hardware and more types of ports for connectivity.

Projected Duty Cycle

Personal computers normally run on 3-year duty cycles. Review your desired duty cycle and make decisions based on this factor. Devices that you wish to run for more years should have as much RAM and flash memory as possible, and be upgradeable if possible. The less expensive devices are turn-key and work very well, but have greater risk of becoming obsolete. Even the lower-end devices will easily give you a 3-year duty cycle and still provide excellent cost and support savings.

Requirements

Review the needs of the users. If you have users that are mostly just coming in and working with software, typing, and doing clerical work, then the cheaper models might be all you need. If the users require additional features like multiple USB ports or 3D graphics, then you might want to look at models with PCI expansion slots. I am strongly of the opinion that it's best to have one model for all users for support reasons, though multiple models if deployed will work fine. Since the software and performance comes from the servers, they will all experience the same functionality.

In-House Expertise

Review your in-house expertise. If you have staff that can customize Linux builds and modify the thin clients, then buy devices that allow for such changes. If you are seeking turn-key solutions, then it might be a good choice to buy a lower-end model. Don't buy too much hardware that will never be used and will only add to the complexity of the project.

Vendor Stability

No matter what device you select, within a few years you will no longer be able to purchase that same physical hardware. But, it's important to know that the company will be around for a while, and will provide support and patches to your hardware. Normally after a period of time, all issues are worked out and no additional patches will be required. Since these devices are not physically running the software, they are not prone to viruses. The patches you will apply in the first few months or year will be related to correcting things that the user community finds and streamlining their use.

Turn-Key versus Customized Solutions

As in-house expertise and scope of deployment are weighed, one must consider multiple factors. Two paths that can be taken are either to use the vendor-supplied turn-key solution or to customize the device and deploy your own version of Linux.

Turn-Key Solution

It is highly recommended that if the turn-key version of Linux provided with the thin clients meets your needs that you deploy initially with that version. The hardware vendors provide excellent capabilities and all of the connection methods will probably be already supported. Most likely, as soon as the thin clients are modified beyond the scope of their original design, your hardware vendor will no longer support their functionality. The hardware vendors know the devices extremely well, and have made the modifications required to make them work in the best possible manner.

Sometimes, however, additional functionality is required, and then a custom version can be initiated. Before taking this step, exhaust the possibility of having the hardware vendor incorporate your ideas or needs into their next release.

Customized Solution

Some of the more expensive thin client devices have so much memory and flash drive space that it is possible to create your own customized version of Linux for deployment. Conditions where this might be considered include the following:

- Software that you wish to run locally on the thin client might be out of date. While normally one doesn't run major packages locally, connectivity packages such as Citrix, Firefox, or Java might need upgrades for functionality or security reasons.

- Some applications that you require for your deployment might not be available from the vendor and will need to be installed via your own build.

- Some applications that are poorly written require unique IP addresses for security reasons, and the back-end software sometimes gets confused when multiple connections are formed from one server. This might happen if all users are accessing software from a GNOME or KDE. These would have to be run locally to circumvent this issue.

- Some hardware features beyond the scope of the vendors design might be implemented. One might want to install PCI devices like 3D video cards, TV tuners, or fibre optic network capabilities into the thin client. This would require modifications to Linux.

When installing Linux on a thin client, there are some issues that need to be considered. While it might be possible to get a significant amount of memory in the hardware, the solid-state flash drives will not have the same capacity as a normal personal computer. Since software is never installed locally, larger flash drives are not needed. However, modern Linux distributions sometimes are difficult to install in this confined space. At the time of writing this book, the largest size of flash drives is 2GB. Fedora Core 6, SLES 10, and Knoppix can be loaded and will run in a 2GB flash drive.

Linux can be installed by multiple methods. One method is to install from a USB memory device. Linux can be booted from a USB drive plugged into the thin client, and then installed to the flash drive contained within the thin client. Another method is to install a USB DVD or CD drive as you would on a personal computer. The Linux distribution will assume the flash drive is a disk drive and install exactly as it does on regular computer hardware.

The following tips will aid you in the installation process:

- You probably will not need a swap device. If the thin client has 512MB or 1GB of memory, it takes a lot of remote applications running to reach that limit. Remember that even if you start up an application like OpenOffice.org, the bulk of the memory footprint is on the server.

- Test the installation first on a regular PC and confirm the installation size there initially, and then re-create the same installation on your thin client. Regular computers will have great performance and the installation process will go faster while you are experimenting.

- During the installation process, de-select all software packages that you will not need. Very little is required normally for thin clients to run. You probably will only need Linux, X-windows, and possible connectivity software such as the Rdesktop client for RDP and the Citrix client for Metaframe.

- Check with your hardware vendor to ensure that custom installs will work on the thin client. Some thin clients have flash devices with a fixed number of writes, and are designed to run on a RAM file system. If this is the case, you need to follow the vendors' recommendation. Always write-protect these file systems to ensure that users do not physically write to the drive, which might happen by accident or on purpose.

- If the flash device is not designed to run with repeated writes, then explore loading distributions like Knoppix, which are designed from the ground up to run in a read-only capacity. In the case of Knoppix, the flash drive is loaded with what normally is loaded on the CD. CDs are read-only and this design is perfectly suited in this case.

Starting the Appropriate Connection Method

Based on your server operating systems, you are now faced with deciding the best connection method to use on the thin clients. If all terminals are using one type of login, it's best to just configure them to boot and connect right to the authentication screens. The fewer steps the users have to do, the better.

XDMCP

XDMCP is supported on most Linux thin clients, and allows you to connect to your GNOME or KDE server. Upon connection the login screen appears and, once the authentication is complete, the thin client will work exactly the same way as the system console.

X-windows works very well on modern networks and provides a crisp and responsive look and feel.

Citrix Metaframe Client

The Citrix client is installed on most thin clients and is available for use. This client is used when bandwidth management is required, and is used on the deployed thin clients when full network speed is not available.

Creating a Chooser for Multiple Connection Methods

Sometimes thin clients are deployed in multiple locations and one type of connection will not be used throughout your organization. The thin client should then allow you to present a "chooser" that will offer users to select the right host to use.

Often, users tend to select the wrong host and avoiding this should be part of your design. For instance, you might have a thin client that uses XDMCP for internal users, and the Citrix client for those are remote sites. So your "chooser" in this case would present two choices. But as you know, your internal users will sometimes click on the Citrix client and vice versa. So, it's best to add some code in the Xsession file that runs before your desktop is started to verify that the user is logging in using the right technology. If they have made an error, produce a simple dialog to exit them off the system.

Personal Computer Hardware Devices

The issue will present itself where certain hardware devices that were previously used on personal computers will have to be deployed or replaced. There are short and long term solutions to re-use your current devices and then moving into the future purchase products better suited for thin-client deployment.

Printers

Many organizations have deployed desktop printers for individual users. However, I feel that this solution is very support-intensive; a far better solution is to use departmental printers that are more robust and networked. This will eliminate them being connected to physical computers and reduce your support costs. USB printers that need to be deployed can be deployed in a number of ways. One way is to purchase a USB extension device and plug it into the server. The server will see it, and add it to the list of available printers. There are also ways that the thin client can be used to pass through jobs to the printer, but this technique is discouraged for the reasons mentioned above. In a larger deployment, cost analysis of the duty cycle of small printers versus a larger networked printer should weigh in favor of the latter.

Scanners

Often, scanners are connected to personal computers for use by employees. Using USB extension technology it should be possible to run the scanner back to the server and all users on that server gain access and scan their items. In my point of view, long term networked scanners should be considered. Also, many photocopiers support the scanning of documents and can send them right into your email server. Email delivery of scanned documents provides a stable, stateless environment that is low in support.

Custom Mice or Keyboards

It's usually a better choice to deploy a consistent mouse and keyboard throughout your organization. This reduces your support costs and ensures that what has been tested in the review process is exactly what the user community will be using. But, sometimes there are situations were users have different types of mice or keyboards for personal or disability reasons. Thankfully, most of these devices are USB-based and should plug right into your thin client and work. Split keyboards and track balls have been tested on thin clients and they work well. The best way to approach this situation is to allow these exceptions with the understanding that any kind of user-added devices are untested and may not work as expected.

Other Desktop Hardware

Sometimes as part of your deployment, there will be circumstances where more robust provision of certain types of hardware cannot be implemented. Software applications might require a specific brand of hardware such as scales or barcode readers via USB or serial ports. In some situations an SCSI device may need to be deployed at a desktop, when the goal is to have the server located in a centralized data centre. Several possibilities exist to deploy these devices:

- SCSI-to-Fibre Optic. Boxes exist that will convert a SCSI port to fibre optic lines and then back to SCSI on the other side. The server is unable to tell the difference and this allows you to deploy this type of hardware at the user desktop

- USB-to-Network. Hardware exists that allows you to place USB on your network. Drivers loaded on the server will fool software into perceiving the connected devices to be local and work correctly.

- Serial-to-Network. Hardware exists that works in the same manner as the USB-to-Network conversion mentioned above. The servers perceive that these serial devices are local to the computer and work as expected.

- Client-Side Device Mapping: Citrix and RDP allow you to map local hardware devices back to the server and the software running on the server will work as expected. For example, a USB device connected to the thin client will appear to be plugged into the server from software and one can access that port.

Enabling Remote Sound

Sound to the thin clients is always an issue that provides problems. The reason for this is because software running on a centralized computer system assumes that the sound should be played on the server. In the figure below you can see the path that sound takes by default. The sound will play in your computer data centre!

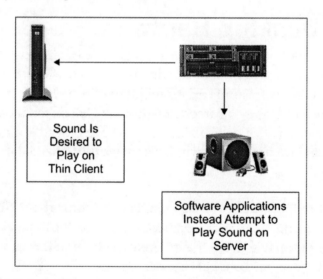

Recently, Linux desktop vendors have started to consider this situation. There are ways to deploy sound so that it plays correctly on the thin clients, but unfortunately no single solution is perfect or will work with all applications. However, you will be able to select applications that will work with your selected sound system and provide the capabilities that you require.

The method for handling this is similar in all such technologies and is diagrammed in the next figure:

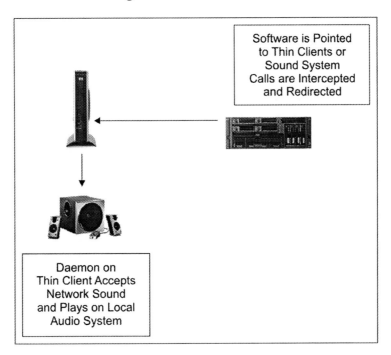

In all cases, a daemon is started on the thin client, which monitors a TCP port for sound requests, and when it receives such a signal it redirects the sound to the sound card or internal speaker of the thin client. On the server side two methods are used for sound redirection. One method involves building software with libraries already designed for such a deployment, and the other is to intercept calls made to the server audio system and redirect them to the appropriate thin client. Decisions are then made on which best meets the needs of your requirements.

NAS—Network Audio System

The network audio system has been available for a number of years and is very stable and works well. Software is built using the NAS libraries and then a daemon on the thin client plays the sounds over the network.

ESD—Esound

Seemingly not under further development, this technology is widely supported and might provide a good fit for your deployment. In a similar manner to NAS, libraries are linked into software that redirects sound to an esound daemon running on the thin client.

Pulse Audio

This project seems to have a high amount of development and might provide an excellent fit for your needs. Many Linux applications already support Pulse Audio and a plug-in is available for the Alsa sound system that will redirect sound to your thin client. Alsa is heavily used on Linux desktops to handle sound requests to the local sound card.

Allowing the Server to Gain Access to USB Devices

Local USB devices that are plugged into a thin client normally will be automatically mounted to the Linux distribution running on that hardware. However, because the user is logged into the server, these devices will not be made available to them. The server will not be aware of this plug-in event and it will not appear on their desktop. If your organization does not want to support USB memory devices, then this condition eliminates the ability of users to upload and download files on such devices. However, most probably you will have to support this hardware. There are certain technologies that allow one to gain access to the USB devices plugged into thin clients via a mount between the server and the local device. While this might work in a small deployment, cases when hundreds of users mount and dismount devices along with their often poor technique might present problems for the server. In such a deployment, a stuck or locked mount might require a complete server reboot to release it. With hundreds of people logged in at a time, obviously this isn't a good solution.

Another option is to use a stateless connection to transfer the files and then once finished, the process is closed and released. One simple method is to use a FTP daemon on the thin client to handle requests. The following figure shows this design in use:

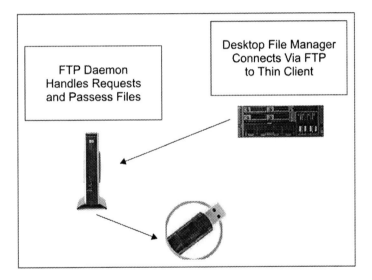

In this design, the home or base directory of the FTP daemon is the same location that USB devices are mounted. Permissions are handled on the server side or via passwords and logging can be enabled on the FTP transfers for later review. The file managers on the desktop (Nautilus in the case of GNOME) support FTP connections, and the user will be presented with a fully graphical solution and not realize the technology procedures for the file transfers. They will simply drop and drag the files, and everything is fully automated.

Summary

You have now deployed the server, the software, and thin clients. These steps have now provided a stable working environment for your users. You have provided them with training, and covered yourself with those in power to ensure that the best possible solution has been deployed. The next chapter will review some ideas for you and your fellow IT staff so that you can better support your organization.

9

Support

When reading a chapter title such as "Support", the first thought that might strike you is probably the consideration for your user community. It goes much deeper than that to encompass the users, multiple tiers of your IT staff, the open-source community, and any software vendors from whom you have purchased software or with whom you have contracts. This chapter will review these various groups in further detail.

Supporting the Users

Supporting the users will be challenging as your users will be working remotely. Various methods are adopted to provide user support including training in order to save the time of your support team and save the users from frustration.

Training

It has already been mentioned previously that the importance of training cannot be underestimated. Each hour that you invest in training will easily be recouped in avoided user frustration and then support from your IT staff. By tracking all calls to the support desk, you will be able to fine-tune later training classes in both content and employees in need of additional skill improvement.

Using VNC to Remotely Control Sessions

The most important tool for supporting users is the ability to see and remotely control their desktop sessions. Most thin clients support the ability to start a VNC daemon. This daemon will run as a service on the operating system of the thin client. When a VNC client is initiated remotely, the daemon will respond to the connection and the users' session will appear on the thin client of your support staff. For this reason, it is recommended that the support group have monitors running at higher resolution than most of your users. For instance, if your users will probably use 1024x768 monitors, then support should run 1152x1024 and up. This will allow the remote-controlled session of the user to entirely fit and not require scrolling to be seen. Once connected, all mouse and keyboard activities can be performed by both people at the same time. One particular client, called "tight VNC" is designed for low-bandwidth connections. This will allow you to control sessions even at your remote sites.

The following figure shows how VNC is used to support the user community.

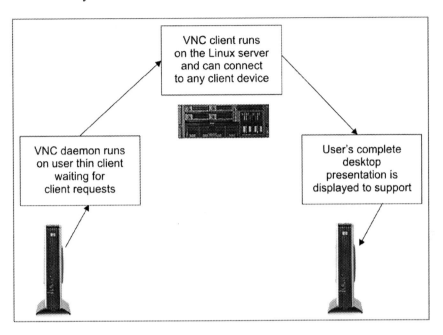

X11tovnc is an excellent program that can be used in the situation where a thin client does not have VNC capabilities locally. It allows all X-windows events to be converted into VNC and, once this is done, the VNC client can be used as described in the figure. The difference is that this utility is run on the server for users whom you want to remotely control.

Vnc2swf is another useful program that is very similar to the VNC client. Once launched, it opens in an identical manner to the regular client. However, it provides the ability to record all screen events and save them to a `.swf` or Shockwave file for later review and analysis. This opens a few very useful features. Firstly, it allows you to record a user's session and watch their actions step by step. Secondly, it can be used to create help screens for the user community. Lastly, it can be used to record software events and then forward them to the open-source community, or support companies for their review. Often, it's far easier to record a session than trying to describe every single step in email.

Screendumps for Analysis

Often there are times when IT support is not available, or something occurs on the desktop when the user cannot immediately contact someone for help. In such situations it helps greatly to provide a method to send print screens to printers and files. If you can allow users to attach screenshots directly to email, then that too would prove very useful. Once the users realize how much easier it is to troubleshoot their issue when the person can see the exact dialog or error message, they will use it frequently.

Custom Help System

The help screens provided with the various software products are often not as robust as the user community will require. In addition, often your organization will have site-specific instructions or techniques that the user community needs for their day-to-day work. It is highly recommended that someone from your support staff be assigned to documentation and create help files for the users in PDF format. Make the files readily available for use on the desktop menus. It is also recommended that the most Frequently Asked Questions (FAQs) be entered into a document as well for their use.

Another method that is effective is to deploy a wiki on your intranet with help topics. This can be configured so that only IT staff can make edits, and also can be deployed in a manner to encourage users to help one another. One gains access to the wiki via a web browser and its very design and nature provides excellent searching and linking.

Support within Your IT Staff

Another aspect is making decisions about how your IT staff will perform the various functions and what kind of people will be responsible for each of the functions. You will probably have to consider the type of support required and then will have to make decisions about moving current staff into slightly different roles and hiring new employees.

Creating the Support Group

Earlier it was mentioned that support is very different on a network of this design. Personal computer networks are very 'middle heavy' with hardware and operating system specialists. Each personal computer desktop that they support requires a great deal of local analysis and tuning. Thin client networks focus staff on future movement and design, and software support.

For software support, anecdotal evidence suggests that one or two people can support approximately 300 concurrent users. Obviously, more people will be required initially, and also during software upgrades. But in a stable day-to-day environment, two people should provide an adequate service level with that many employees. They will take all initial calls, and answer the bulk of questions, drawing from acquired lists of Frequently Asked Questions. In the event of an issue that they cannot resolve, the information will be passed to the next level, which is normally a Systems Administrator. Because the thin clients can be swapped upon failure, normally the software support staff can also replace hardware for your organization. Though thin clients rarely fail, the keyboards, mice, and monitors start to have failures after approximately the third year.

One or two System Administrators can support approximately 300 concurrent users. This includes installing upgrades, monitoring servers, developing new technology, and taking issues forwarded from your software support staff. These staff should be intimate with the design and layout of the servers and will be called upon to support unusual issues as they arise.

It's very important to create an environment where users clearly understand that all calls should be created with the software support staff, and that the Systems Administrators should not be called directly. Sometimes it's frustrating for the user community, because they know the Admin will be able to resolve their call quickly and immediately. However, this is not good use of staff time. Users should never select staff to call for support as this should be handled by internal procedures.

Training

Just as it is important to train your users, it's important to keep the skills of your support staff energized and current. The software support staff should sit in user training classes and follow the learning curve to the highest level possible. The System Administrators should be given opportunities to go to training classes. It also is greatly helpful to allow them to attend seminars and conventions that present technology previews. Vendors will demonstrate new technology, which can be used to streamline your design or add additional functionality in the future.

Logging All Calls

It's very important to log all calls that you receive. Previously it was mentioned that the 'Preps' software application can be used on Linux for this function. Preps provides a very simple interface for note taking and assigning issues. Data accumulated from your call-taking software should be used to generate your Frequently Asked Questions, and also to tune the size of your staff. It's difficult to ask for increases in staff size without detailed information and therefore every call being logged is very important, even if the call is quickly answered.

Vendor and Open-Source Support

We have seen how you provide support to your users and within your IT team. But what if you need support! If the need arises, you can always turn to your vendor or the open-source community for support.

Selecting Vendor Support Level

As you select the operating systems to deploy, one major consideration is the skills of your staff. Some operating systems can be deployed for 'free' and are only supported via the open-source community with no service levels for problem resolution. I have had success in deploying some 'lesser-supported' operating systems in areas that are not mission critical. Linux is extremely stable in any form, and one normally has excellent results with community builds, but weigh these issues before you deploy. Operating system vendors such as Red Hat, Canonical, or Novell provide support on server and desktop flavors of Linux. They also have different levels of support and response times. The more you pay, the faster the response and the greater number of hours that support is available during the day.

Interacting with the Vendor

Vendor support can sometimes be very frustrating. If you have worked in the computer field previously, you know this to be true of all operating systems and types of computers.

Assign one person to be in charge of contacting the vendor. Often, the support contract will require only one contact, but take all the steps possible to make sure that multiple employees are not contacting the vendor for the same problems. This not only wastes time on your side, but on the vendor's side as well.

It's very important to ensure that you have complete information before contacting the vendor's support group. Just as you yourself have set up multiple tiers of support, they will have done the same thing. The first level of support will normally ask basic questions, and almost always ask you to ensure that your patch levels on packages are current. The first thing that you will always want to do is check the vendor download sites for upgrades and install them as needed. Hopefully, your problem is resolved with the upgrade; but often this is not the case. You will then get to the second tier of support, and they will be more useful in resolving your problem. If you can replicate the bug or issue, make sure you give the exact steps required to cause the failure.

Most Linux applications will produce crash dumps upon failure. In the GNOME desktop, bug-buddy is normally tripped and will produce a lot of the crash information that is often very useful for the vendor or open-source developers. It is recommended that you train your users to save this output to files and then contact your internal support group for processing. The next two figures show bug buddy being activated upon software failure, the steps required to save the information to a flat file.

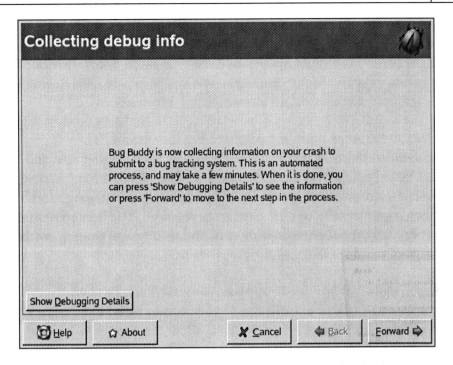

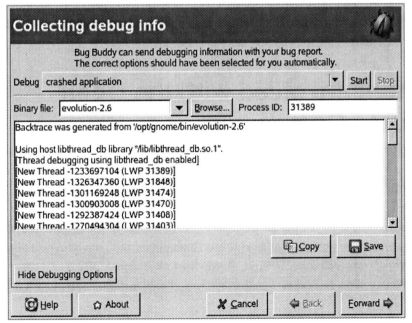

Your support staff will be able to ask the right questions, and create a more complete bug report than the users. Bug reports allow you to attach crash data and that should always be done if possible. Some distributions have packages with "debug" in their name, and these are used during the debugging process to produce more detailed information.

Be very careful when applying patches from the vendor. It is recommended that you use an old computer as your staging area and always install patches on that machine first. Take the operating system media from a production server and recreate it on your staging machine and then incrementally test the patches as required. The user community is not very tolerant of enterprise failures and testing and staging patches allows you to reduce risk.

The same tools that you use to support your users can be used to provide more useful information to your vendors and the open-source community. When possible, allow the vendor to log into your network with remote control protocols like Citrix or VNC. You can also use VNC to remote control their session and show them exactly how the software failure occurs. It's also useful to record crashes using vnc2swf and send them the resulting Flash files.

Getting Involved with the Open Source Community

Interestingly, there have been many times that the open-source community has provided better support and faster fixes than support provided by software vendors. Many of the projects are a product of passion, and the developers are very interested in the quality of their code and fixing bugs. In the same way that you provide work files and debug logs to vendors, you can submit them to the open-source community. Most major projects like Firefox, Evolution, and OpenOffice.org have community sites for entering and tracking bugs and requesting features.

Another interesting option is to create a bounty page of fixes or features that you wish to expedite. It is sometimes possible to define certain specific software changes and a monetary value for that alteration. Many open-source developers are youngsters eager for work, and will gladly work with you on your issues.

Most major open-source projects have an IRC channel where developers and users communicate for reasons of support and conversation. Be respectful of channel rules, and you will find that people generally are very friendly and will provide help to you for your questions. Some projects have unique user and development channels. In this case, make sure that you ask the right questions in the correct places. There is a wealth of information on the IRC and it's one of the best methods for real-time interaction concerning your deployed applications.

Summary

You now have some ideas and direction in the area of support. The quality of support you provide to your users will directly reflect in the success of your deployment. Likewise, the quality of information that you provide to your vendors will reduce the amount of time required to get issues resolved.

Resources

The URLs of the various projects and hardware mentioned in this book have been listed together in this appendix.

- Airspeak Thin Clients
  http://www.airspeak.com/

- Beagle File Search System
  http://beagle-project.org/Main_Page

- Beryl 3D Session Manager
  http://beryl-project.org

- Citrix Connection Client
  http://www.citrix.com

- Evolution Email Client
  http://www.gnome.org/projects/evolution/

- Firefox Web Browser
  http://www.mozilla.com/en-US/firefox/

- F- Spot Picture Processor
  http://f-spot.org/Main_Page

- GAIM Instant Messenger

  `http://gaim.sourceforge.net/`

- GIMP Graphic Editor

  `http://www.gimp.org/`

- GNOME Desktop

  `http://www.gnome.org/`

- HP Thin Clients

  `http://www.hp.com/`

- Inkscape SVG Editor

  `http://www.inkscape.org/`

- KDE Desktop

  `http://www.kde.org/`

- LTSP — Linux Terminal Server Project

  `http://www.ltsp.org/`

- Mail Notification

  `http://www.nongnu.org/mailnotify/`

- Mono .Net Runtime

  `http://www.mono-project.com/Main_Page`

- MySQL Database

  `http://www.mysql.org/`

- NAS Audio System

  `http://www.radscan.com/nas.html`

- Neoware Thin Clients

  `http://www.neoware.com/`

- OpenOffice.org Suite

  `http://www.openoffice.org/`

- Planner Project Management System

  `http://live.gnome.org/Planner`

- Postgre Database

  `http://www.postgresql.org/`

- Pulse Audio System

  `http://pulseaudio.org/`

- Realplayer Audio/Video Player

  `http://www.real.com/`

- Rdesktop RDP Client

  `http://www.rdesktop.org/`

- Tomboy Note Taker

  `http://www.gnome.org/projects/tomboy/`

- X3270 Emulation

  `http://x3270.bgp.nu/`

- Xine Audio /Video Player

  `http://xinehq.de/`

B
Installing
OpenSUSE 10.2

Many of the examples in this book, and in fact nowadays, the next generation desktop servers are developed on OpenSUSE 10.2. Other Linux distributions will have strengths and weaknesses that you should consider while handling the deployment. The instructions that follow are meant to guide you through the installation process of OpenSUSE 10.2. Later version of OpenSUSE and other distributions in general will be similar.

You will want to download the ISO from `http://www.opensuse.org` and burn a DVD. Remember that downloading a full distribution meant for DVD will possibly take a good amount of time.

The following steps will guide you through your installation process:

1. Insert the DVD into the computer on which you want to install the operating system. It's best not to attempt this on a machine used for current production work. One might be tempted to install it on a computer already running Microsoft Windows. But it is better to load it on a computer that can be dedicated for testing and can be reloaded multiple times if required. After you have completed your testing, the same procedures will be used to install the operating system on a permanent server.

2. Ensure that the computer is configured in the BIOS to boot from the DVD drive before attempting to gain access to the hard drive.

3. Boot the computer, and the OpenSUSE installation menu will appear. Note that the first option on the list is to **Boot from Hard Drive**. It will attempt to do this after a few seconds.

4. Arrow once down to **Installation** and it will pause and allow you to configure additional settings. From this screen you can make changes to the resolution if desired. Pressing *Enter* will allow you to continue.

5. The installer version of Linux will boot from the DVD and this might take a minute or two to complete. X will eventually attempt to start and the screen will change from character to graphical.

6. The first screen that appears is the language selection screen. Navigate to your desired language and select **Next**.

7. The next screen is where one accepts the license, after doing so select **Next**.

8. The **Installation Mode** screen will allow you to select **New Installation**, which will perform a fresh install. Select **Next**.

9. The **Clock and Time Zone** screen allows you to configure your time zone. Select the appropriate region and time zone, and then press **Next**.

10. From the **Desktop Selection** screen select either the **GNOME** or **KDE** desktop for installation. The examples provided in this book are based on the GNOME desktop. Once the desktop has been selected, press **Next**.

11. The **Installation Settings** screen appears, and allows you to fine tune the installation process. Clicking on **Partitioning** provides you with the ability to fine-tune the file system sizes used during the installation process. It also will allow you to configure the swap device, which is used when system physical memory is depleted. For testing purposes, the default settings will work fine. Your final server installation will probably require some custom settings.

12. From the **Installation Settings** screen, select the **Software** option.

13. This screen allows you to customize the exact packages that you wish to install in addition to the base desktop that you already selected. Very likely, you will want to add some additional network services and it's always good to install the development packages. If installing the GNOME desktop, it is recommended to add **Console Tools, File Server, Print Server, Network Administration, Mail and News Server, Basis Development, GNOME Development, C/C++ Development, Linux Kernel Development, Perl Development**, and **Python Development**. Once finished click **OK Accept**.

14. Possibly, you will have to accept their licenses, to do so.

15. A dialog may appear alerting you to the packages that will be installed. Press **Continue**.

16. You will return to the **Installation Settings** screen and press **Accept** to continue.

17. You will be given one last warning concerning your impending installation to the computer. If you are ready to install, click on **Install**.

18. Your hard drive will then be partitioned, and once this has completed the software installation process will begin.

19. Once completed, the computer will reboot; allow it to **Boot from Hard Disk**.

20. The **Password for the System Administrator "root"** screen will then appear. Enter the desired password for this account and click **Next**.

21. On the **Hostname and Domain Name** screen, assign the computer a name, and click **Next**.

22. The **Network Configuration** screen allows you to configure your connectivity and configure the software firewall. Based on your network design, you can have the machine assigned a number via DHCP or enter a static IP address. Once finished, select **Next**.

23. The **Test Internet Connection** screen allows you to verify your connectivity to the Internet if desired. This is not required to complete the operating system installation. Selecting **No, Skip This Test** and **Next** will continue to the next screen.

24. The **User Authentication Method** screen is where you can configure password validation for user logins. For your initial testing you will probably want to select **Local /etc/password**. Optionally, it can be configured to use LDAP, NIS, or a Windows Domain. Once you have made your selection, click on **Next**.

25. The screen **New Local User** appears, and this allows you to add a regular user account. You will want to use a regular user account during the testing process to ensure that protections are correct for the user community. Uncheck the setting **Automatic Login** so that the login screen appears. Otherwise, this named user is automatically logged into the computer without any passwords. Select **Next** when finished.

26. The **Release Notes** will appear, select **Next** when you are ready to continue.

27. The **Hardware Configuration** screen will take a few seconds to display. Linux makes an attempt to locate your video card, monitor, and connected hardware. From this screen you can make minor adjustments to the settings if required. Most probably, you won't have to change anything. Select **Next**.

28. The **Installation Completed** screen appears. Select **Finish**.

At this point the computer will activate additional services and boot into graphical mode. It is now ready for testing and to implement the custom changes that are described in the chapters.

Index

memory management 9
misconceptions 14
multi tasking 12
references 147
software compatibility 8
types 19
versus client/server 34
thin clients versus client/server 34
Tomboy 105
Total Cost of Ownership 31
turn key solution
about 123
versus customized solutions 123
types, thin clients
handheld devices 27
Linux devices 23
proprietary operating systems 19
Windows embedded devices 21
wireless devices 25

U

UNIX based servers
gnome-terminal 115
xterm 116
user community issues
about 42
application training 44
communication 42
desktop bling 45
desktop training 43
initial feedback 42
issue tracking software 45
open source CDs 46
user support
about 135
custom help system 138

remote control sessions, VNC used
136-138
screendumps, analyzing 138
training 135

V

vendor support
about 141
open source community 144, 145
support level, selecting 141
vendor, interacting with 142, 144
video processors
Real Player 113
Xine 112

W

Windows application
connecting to 117
Windows embedded devices 21
wireless devices
about 25
advantages 26
disadvantages 26

X

XDMCP
about 127
authentication methods 78
custom login screen, creating 65, 68
custom splash screen, creating 69, 70
enabling 64
login screen enabling, gdmsetup used
70-77
Xine 112
xterm 116

Thank you for buying
Linux Thin Client Networks
Design and Deployment

Packt Open Source Project Royalties

When we sell a book written on an Open Source project, we pay a royalty directly to that project.

In the long term, we see ourselves and you—customers and readers of our books—as part of the Open Source ecosystem, providing sustainable revenue for the projects we publish on. Our aim at Packt is to establish publishing royalties as an essential part of the service and support a business model that sustains Open Source.

If you're working with an Open Source project that you would like us to publish on, and subsequently pay royalties to, please get in touch with us.

Writing for Packt

We welcome all inquiries from people who are interested in authoring. Book proposals should be sent to authors@packtpub.com. If your book idea is still at an early stage and you would like to discuss it first before writing a formal book proposal, contact us; one of our commissioning editors will get in touch with you.

We're not just looking for published authors; if you have strong technical skills but no writing experience, our experienced editors can help you develop a writing career, or simply get some additional reward for your expertise.

About Packt Publishing

Packt, pronounced 'packed', published its first book "Mastering phpMyAdmin for Effective MySQL Management" in April 2004 and subsequently continued to specialize in publishing highly focused books on specific technologies and solutions.

Our books and publications share the experiences of your fellow IT professionals in adapting and customizing today's systems, applications, and frameworks. Our solution-based books give you the knowledge and power to customize the software and technologies you're using to get the job done. Packt books are more specific and less general than the IT books you have seen in the past. Our unique business model allows us to bring you more focused information, giving you more of what you need to know, and less of what you don't.

Packt is a modern, yet unique publishing company, which focuses on producing quality, cutting-edge books for communities of developers, administrators, and newbies alike. For more information, please visit our website: www.PacktPub.com.

OpenVPN: Building and Integrating Virtual Private Networks

ISBN: 1-904811-85-X   Paperback: 258 pages

Learn how to build secure VPNs using this powerful Open Source application

1. Learn how to install, configure, and create tunnels with OpenVPN on Linux, Windows, and MacOSX

2. Use OpenVPN with DHCP, routers, firewall, and HTTP proxy servers

3. Advanced management of security certificates

Hacking Vim: A Cookbook to get the Most out of the Latest Vim Editor

ISBN: 978-1-847190-93-2   Paperback: 228 pages

From personalizing Vim to productivity optimizations: Recipes to make life easier for experienced Vim users

1. Create, install, and use Vim scripts

2. Personalize your work-area

3. Optimize your Vim editor to be faster and more responsive

Printed in the United Kingdom
by Lightning Source UK Ltd.
123144UK00001B/61-80/A